Jails to Jobs:

SEVEN STEPS TO BECOMING EMPLOYED

Dedication

To Carol, my beloved wife, for the love, support, patience, kindness and generosity she offers me each and every day. I am so lucky and grateful beyond words.

This book is also dedicated to the memory of my dear mother, Gene Drevno, an incredible role model to me and each of my eight brothers and sisters. Tragically widowed at the age of 43, she re-entered the workforce and labored tirelessly for 32 years attending to the needs of the disadvantaged people she served. Those she touched knew they were not alone and that she would never turn away from them. She is, and will always remain, my hero.

Acknowledgment

Heartfelt thanks and acknowledgment goes to Judy Jacobs for the countless hours she devoted to this project. She took my ideas and words, tirelessly developing, editing and rewriting. Her generosity, care and expertise are woven throughout the pages of this book. Without her efforts, this book would never have been published. It has been a real privilege for me to work with her, and I offer her my deepest gratitude and appreciation.

SEVEN STEPS TO BECOMING EMPLOYED

By Mark Drevno

Library of Congress Cataloging-in-Publication Data is available.

For further information on this book, workshops, classes and speaking engagements contact: info@jailstojobs.org

Connect with Jails to Jobs at: www.jailstojobs.org

ISBN 978-0-9912197-0-4

All of the net proceeds from the sale of this book go to Jails to Jobs, Inc., a Section 501 (c) (3) public charity, to fund its work in supporting soon-to-be-released inmates, ex-offenders, their families and communities and ultimately reducing recidivism and improving public safety.

Published by:
Jails to Jobs, Inc.
3641 Mount Diablo Blvd., #1164
Lafayette, CA 94549

Book design: Ianziti Design
Indexer: Ty Koontz

Please note: Although the contact info in this book primarily targets the San Francisco Bay Area, you can find organizations similar to those listed throughout the United States. Your local American Job Center (www.servicelocator.org) and public library (www.publiclibraries.com) can help you locate them. Also, your local public community college career center (www.utexas.edu/world/comcol/state) can be helpful and should be open to the public, whether you're enrolled as a student or not.

Table of Contents

The search begins

"We are all potential criminals, and those who we have put into prison are no worse, deep down, than any one of us. They have succumbed to ignorance, desire and anger, ailments that we all suffer from but to different degrees. Our duty is to help them."

–His Holiness, The Dalai Lama

Many of you who are reading this book have been out of the job market for a long time. And, as ex-offenders, you will have additional challenges to face as you begin your search for employment. But don't be discouraged.

You all have special skills to offer a potential employer. You also have abilities and talent that companies both large and small are looking for. The key is to find those employers and convince them to hire you. That is what this book is all about.

We have developed a step-by-step approach, called "my new entry," that will take you through the process of finding a job. We offer tips and techniques to help you be more effective and give you the encouragement you need to reach your final goal—a job that is a good fit for you and an employer who respects you as a worker.

In preparing this book, we have drawn inspiration from some of the best job search and marketing experts in the nation, including Richard Bolles, Marty Nemko, Larry Robbin and the late Jay Conrad Levinson. We owe them a debt of gratitude for all the help they have given to job seekers over the years and for what we have learned from them.

As you look for and find a job, we would love to hear from you. Tell us your stories, and we may be able to include some of them on our website, www.jailstojobs.org. Send an email to info@jailstojobs.org, and let us know how the methods outlined in this book helped you in your job search and what sorts of successes you have achieved. Your stories could help other ex-offenders, who may have situations similar to your own. Through sharing experiences, we hope to create a forum that will serve people who are at all steps of the journey toward getting a job.

Good luck.

STEP 1

Getting started

"It doesn't matter where you are coming from. All that matters is where you are going." – Brian Tracy, self-help author, speaker and lecturer

Before you can even begin to look for a job, you need to do a lot of preparation.

Set the stage. Looking for a job is like acting in a play or a movie. First you need to set the stage so that you will have the right attitude, the proper image and the appropriate lines to speak. After you have done that, it's time to go and meet your audience. Your audience is potential employers and anyone else who can help you find a job.

Be a star. You are the star of your job search and can play your role in whatever way you please. Plan your plot and the way you will carry it out and practice, practice and practice some more. It is only through practicing that you will get the courage and the confidence to go on stage—whether in an interview or by showing up at a company unannounced.

Getting to know yourself

The first thing you need to do is get to know yourself a bit better and learn your strengths and weaknesses. Doing this will give you a better sense of the kinds of jobs that will be suitable for you.

Aim higher. You may not want to be the person you were in the past—the one who got in trouble and was incarcerated. Deep down you know that you are much better than that and have the skills, abilities and dedication that employers are looking for.

Take tests. Perhaps the best way to learn more about your personality traits and abilities is to take various types of assessment tests. There are many of these available online. Some cost money. Others are free. You can also take these tests at an American Job Center.

Finding help

American Job Centers. These centers, formally known as One-Stop Career Centers, are sponsored by the U.S. Department of Labor and are located throughout all 50 states, as well as in Puerto Rico and the U.S. Virgin Islands. Many urban areas have multiple locations to help as many job seekers as possible.

Free services. Depending on the particular location, American Job Centers offer a variety of services. Once you register at one of them, you can go there as often as you like. These places are incredibly useful for job seekers and have been set up to help people like you find a job. They have high-speed Internet access, fax machines, photocopiers and phones to use free of charge. In fact, nothing the centers do costs anything.

They offer a wide variety of workshops on various aspects of job searching. You can find listings of current job openings, and there are on-site employer hiring events.

The American Job Centers also give a variety of tests and surveys that will assess your skills, aptitudes, interests and personality. And the people who work there can help you figure out the meaning of the results of these tests and what to do with what you have learned from them.

Job leads and training. At an American Job Center, you can also find job leads and get help with career planning, job training and transition solutions to re-enter the workforce. Many of them have special programs and job counselors to help ex-offenders, veterans and the disabled. The counselors can tell you about training programs and whether you might qualify for any federal or state money available to pay for them. You can also get referrals to community services and resources.

The American Job Centers are designed to do everything they can to help you find a job. So if you live near one, definitely check it out. You can find your local Center by going online at www.jobcenter.usa.gov or by calling 877-872-5627.

If you can't use the Internet

Many of the ways of finding help and information that are discussed in this book require using the Internet, but using the Internet can be a parole violation for some ex-offenders. If this applies to you, there are plenty of other ways to look for a job, and these are discussed in this book. Rather than using online searches to find potential employers, for example, you can use the telephone Yellow Pages and the type of business directories that most libraries have. Ask your local librarian or American Job Center counselor for help.

Exploring careers

Once you've taken a personal assessment test and know your strengths and weaknesses and what type of job may be suitable for you, it's time to find out more about those jobs.

There are many resources online to explore careers, job markets in various states, and training programs. The websites below are the ones we've found to be most useful.

Occupational Outlook Handbook (www.bls.gov/ooh). One of the best ways to learn about different jobs is by checking out the Occupational Outlook Handbook published by the U.S. Department of Labor's Bureau of Labor Statistics. This handbook is full of information on hundreds of types of jobs. It includes descriptions of what workers do and the working conditions for a particular job, the training and education required for that job, how much you can expect to earn and what the job prospects are.

It includes links to trade organizations where you can find out more information about education and training opportunities. It also has a link to O*Net, where you can find out the average salary—annually or hourly depending on the type of position—for the job, both nationwide and, in some cases, in various states.

O*Net (www.onetonline.org). O*Net, another Department of Labor resource, offers information about various jobs. This information includes the tasks you would perform in a particular job, the environment you would perform it in, the tools you would use, and the knowledge, skills, abilities and education needed for that job.

CareerInfoNet (www.careerinfonet.com). This site, yet another service of the U.S. Department of Labor's CareerOneStop, supplies extensive information on occupations, industries and state labor markets and includes helpful videos about what some of the jobs are like, as well as lists of training opportunities and how to finance them.

Search online. Another way to find out about careers is to use a search engine and search for the name of the career you're interested in plus "careers"—for example "carpenter careers," "construction careers" or "retail careers."

You can also go to Indeed.com and search using a skill you'd like to use in a job, for example framing, driving, forklift operating, customer service, cooking or whatever. Pick out one or two careers you think are interesting. Then search Amazon for books on those careers. Try to find a book that includes people's stories on what it's like to work in that career. If you find one you want to explore further, check your local library's online catalog to see if it's available, so you don't have to buy it.

Transfer your skills. If you have had work experience and want to know what other jobs you can do with the skills you've developed, go to www.myskillsmyfuture.org, put the name of the jobs you have done, and it will tell you other jobs that require those same skills. You can compare careers, find training and search for jobs.

After you decide which career you might be interested in, ask around to locate some people who work in that field. Call them to request an informational interview, so you can learn more about the job from people who actually do it. You'll learn more about how to do an informational interview in Step 4 of this book.

Decide what you want. It can't be stressed enough that you must be clear to yourself about what you want. Don't just look for any job. Decide what you really like to do. Determine your passion and go for it. Then approach employers who have that type of work. Remember that you will be working eight hours a day or longer, so make sure the job will be something that's a reasonable fit. Also remember that employers don't like to hear "I'm open to anything," or "I'll do anything." This may make you look like you're not really serious or you're desperate.

Thinking positive

You're not going to get anywhere with a negative attitude. Although you've made mistakes, you have already done your time and are ready for a new life.

Focus on your strengths and what is right about you. Don't concentrate on the negative stuff. Doing that will just provide another hurdle to overcome.

Improve your image. Start the day by looking in the mirror with a smile and giving yourself a pep talk. The way you see and think about yourself is extremely important. If you think that you are competent and can do a good job, no matter what it is, other people will think so too. It's all about the image you project. Make it a positive, confident and pleasant one.

Concentrate on the good. Jon Kabat-Zinn, who was a professor of medicine and the founding director of the Stress Reduction Clinic and the Center for Mindfulness in Medicine, Health Care, and Society at the University of Massachusetts Medical School, has some excellent advice. He says: "*There is more right with you than wrong with you, even if you are sick or troubled or in pain and things in your life feel dark and out of control. What is 'right' with you holds the key for regaining control of your life and growing beyond your problems.*" Concentrate on what is right.

Try positive self-talk. Learn to do what some people call positive self-talk. This is a type of positive thinking that is also known as an affirmation. Positive thoughts can rewire our thinking and reinforce positive attitudes. Like my old teacher used to say, "*I think I can, I think I can, I know I can, I will!*"

Try it sometime. For example, say something like: "*I will find a job. My good-natured attitude is contagious to everyone I meet. I take the actions needed for success each day. My positive actions attract people and money to me. If it is to be, it is up to me.*" Write your own phrase.

Write down affirmations on index cards or pieces of paper, and choose a new one each day. Say it 10 times, several times a day while job hunting. Say one before you begin making your cold calls and while you are filling out applications, emailing resumes or on your way in the door to an interview. Feel the power they can give you! They will change the way you think about yourself.

Adjusting your attitude

One thing to remember is not to "act jobless." Don't think in terms of being unemployed or looking for work, and don't ever include those types of words in your vocabulary. Instead you are in the process of exploring a new career or a career change. That mindset makes you more confident. It also makes the process seem like an effort to improve your life—not just find a job.

Foolish confidence

Being foolishly confident is a good idea in most cases. It may seem foolish to act like you know a bit more than you actually do, but that will give the potential employer a good impression of you. Your enthusiasm for your own talent will help sell yourself and make your abilities come to life. In many cases, when you start out you are an impostor. When you are a beginner you have to fake it until you make it.

Cleaning up your virtual image

What potential employers find out about you online can seriously hurt you in your job search. Many people are careless with their Facebook, Twitter and YouTube accounts. They post photos and write comments that might make hiring managers think twice about whether they would make good future employees.

Maybe they're holding a beer and look like they've had a bit too much to drink, or say so in a posting. Maybe they're getting a little too personal with their boyfriend or are wearing a bikini or other revealing clothing. Or maybe they're showing off a new tattoo.

Facebook and Twitter aren't the only sites where someone could find questionable information about you. Who knows what they might find if they Google your name? And about 79% of employers search the Internet to screen potential employees.

Google yourself. Be sure to Google yourself and review everything the search engine pulls up about you. If you have created pages or allowed others to post on social networking sites such as Facebook or YouTube, make sure you check them out very carefully. Look for questionable photos and four-letter words that would scare off hiring managers.

Check out of Facebook. In order to be safe, you may want to be like many job seekers these days and deactivate your Facebook account. That way, you won't get into trouble with potential employers who may not like what they see on that popular social networking site. (And you can never be sure what they might not like.) You can deactivate your Facebook account by going to "account settings" and following the directions.

Once you find a job, you can go in and reactivate your account without losing anything that was in it. You still may want to clean it up, however—and be very careful about what goes up on social media sites. You never know when your boss might want to check on what you're doing outside of work and what you might typically say to your friends. Be very wary.

When it comes to social media, it's better to be safe than sorry. There have been several major studies done in which the majority of employers reported that they decided not to hire candidates because of what they found out about them online.

Tattoo removal

Remove antisocial and/or gang related tattoos, and your chances of finding a job will be dramatically increased. In fact, Father Boyle, who founded Homeboy Industries in Los Angeles, said the greatest impediment that those with these types of tattoos face in their job search is the very tattoos themselves.

Just think about it from an employer's perspective. Whether they're gang related or just decorative, visible tattoos may make coworkers feel uncomfortable, scare off customers or give an impression of unprofessionalism.

Laser tattoo removal will drastically reduce job discrimination and casual interest by police and can also help prevent random violence. In addition, it will increase your self-esteem and be part of the life changes you want to make.

Research for a 2011 report published by Project New Start, an Oakland, Calif.-based program for at-risk youth who want to have their tattoos removed, found they wanted to do so for the following reasons:

- To make a positive change or a new start
- To avoid violence or to become an ex–gang member
- For professional reasons (e.g. to get a job)
- To remove the mistake
- The desire to be a role model

Many studies have found that many people who got tattoos were sorry later. Don't be sorry about that tattoo. Do something about it.

These days, tattoos are removed by lasers, which break down the pigment so it's absorbed by the skin. The process may take a number of sessions, and like getting the tattoo itself, can be a bit painful. Removal can also be expensive, but many organizations and local governments offer free tattoo removal for ex-gang members, ex-offenders and others.

For an online directory of low-cost and free tattoo removal programs across the United States, go to www.jailstojobs.org and click on the tattoo removal icon.

Choosing the right email address and voice-mail message

Since most people use email these days, you must have an email address. Otherwise you don't look professional. And most companies who post job listings want applicants to communicate by email in addition to the telephone.

Choose an appropriate email address. Be sure your email address is simple and straightforward. Don't use slang or double meanings. Your name makes the best address. You can use your first and last name if it's unusual. Or you can use your first and last name and middle initial or your first initial and last name. If these are already taken, add some numbers.

If you don't have a computer, you can visit an American Job Center or your local public library and use theirs. You'll need to visit on a regular basis—at least every other day—to check responses to the email messages you send out.

Prepare a proper voice-mail message. Another thing you must have is a professional sounding voice-mail message, so hiring managers will get a good impression when they call. Make sure it is short and sweet. Don't include a portion of your favorite song or something you think is clever. Be sure to use your real first name and not an inappropriate nickname. Just say *"Hi, this is (your name—first and last). I'm not available right now. Please leave me your telephone number and a message, and I'll get back to you as soon as I can. Thank you."*

Creating a 15-second elevator pitch

Everyone looking for a job needs what is known as an elevator pitch. An elevator pitch is a sales pitch about yourself and what you would bring to a job—a kind of advertisement about you. People call it an elevator pitch, because it can be delivered in the time it would take to ride an elevator between a few floors.

Practice your pitch. By creating an elevator pitch and practicing it over and over again, you will have something to use in interviews when asked *"Tell me about yourself."* You can also use your pitch as an introduction for cold calls, when you contact a potential employer you might find on the Internet or in the telephone Yellow Pages.

Keep it to the point. Make your elevator pitch no more than 30 seconds, but most people say about 15 seconds is best. You should be able to cover the essential information in that amount of time. Include what you are able to do and how your skills will benefit an employer. Most people have at least 30 skills that can benefit an employer. What are yours?

Check out these 15-second elevator pitches:

Hello, my name is John Smith, and I have 10 years experience as a forklift driver in the warehouses of several manufacturing companies. I am experienced in machinery maintenance and warehouse stocking, have a California forklift certification and have a passion for helping companies improve their warehouse management. I am looking for a medium-sized company, preferably in the East Bay, where I can contribute my talent.

Hello, my name is Spencer Brown and I have five years experience as a carpenter specializing in residential construction and remodeling. I have knowledge of many building trades, can do framing and door and window installation, have experience in bathroom remodels and can read and understand blueprints. I am hard-working and reliable and get along well with clients and co-workers. I also speak Spanish with a fair amount of fluency. And I love what I do.

Creating a job search team

Building a job search team can help you dramatically expand your reach and find more opportunities. It may take awhile to do this, but the payoff can be tremendous.

Although estimates vary, it is believed that only a small portion of the available jobs are actually advertised. This may be especially true of the small companies that hire most of the people in this country. They use their employees, their friends and their acquaintances to recommend people for them to hire.

Choose members wisely. You must take the same approach that small companies do. Create a job search team. This team will be your troop, your eyes and ears on the ground as you scour the landscape for potential opportunities. Choose a group of not more than 10 people who know you and your abilities well. These must be people who really like you and are willing to take the time to help you achieve your goal of finding a job. They may be former co-workers who thought you were great, bosses for whom you did a good job, family members, friends, ministers or whomever. Ideally your team members will be doing the type of job you want to do, since they will be more likely to learn of opportunities.

Make face-to-face contact. Carefully decide how you want to approach each potential team member, and if possible, get together with them in person. If you can afford it, take them out for coffee. When you call to invite them, make it clear that you're not going to ask them for a job, rather you just want some guidance on your search. When you do get together, tell them in detail your situation and what type of job you are looking for. Ask them if they *"know someone who might know someone"* who might be looking to hire a person with your qualifications, either now or in the future.

If they say no, ask them if they would keep their ears open for potential opportunities for you. Also ask them if they would mind if you called them back in a month or so to check in. In almost all cases, the people you choose are willing to cooperate, since they are people you know well and care about you. That is why you chose them in the first place.

Keep notes. It helps to keep a record of your members and what they have told you. Buy a file box and a set of index cards. Or just use a pad of paper. Put the name of each member of your team at the top of a card and then make a list of the dates you talked to them and what they said. You can also do this on a computer, using a Word document or an Excel spreadsheet, if you have the knowledge to do that. It will also help to keep a calendar. After you talk to each member, schedule your next call to them on a day the following month.

Top tips from employers

Harris International surveyed 2,298 U.S. hiring managers and human resource professionals in 2012 and found that 51 percent reported that their organizations have at one time hired someone with a criminal record.

Conducted on behalf of CareerBuilder, which operates the www.careerbuilder.com job search website, the survey asked the employers who responded to recommend what ex-offenders can do to make themselves more marketable in the job market.

In order of importance, these are:

- Be up-front and honest about the conviction, and stress what you learned from it (68 percent).
- Be willing to work your way up (48 percent).
- Stay positive (46 percent).
- Prepare while you're in prison by taking classes or getting a degree or vocational training (39 percent).
- Don't apply to jobs where your record would automatically disqualify you (31 percent).
- Volunteer (31 percent).
- Take freelance or temporary assignments (26 percent).
- Consider joining the military (18 percent).
- Start your own business (16 percent).
- Monitor what is said on social media (13 percent).

According to the U.S. Dept. of Justice, nearly 40 percent of America's working-age adult population has a criminal record. Refusing to hire anyone with a record significantly decreases the number of applicants for hire and can be criminally wrong itself, unless it is a legitimate business disqualification.

STEP 2

Beginning the job of finding a job

"You are always a valuable, worthwhile human being, not because anybody says so, not because you're successful, not because you make a lot of money, but because you decide to believe it and for no other reason."

— Wayne Dyer, personal development author and speaker

The best time to start your job search is right now. Not tomorrow. Not next week, but now.

Some people think that certain times of the year are better for job searching. That may be true, but there are always jobs available. Even if companies are not creating new jobs because of a bad economy, there will be job openings. People retire. They get fired. They leave for another job. They go on maternity leave. There are a lot of reasons why jobs might come onto the market. And job openings can happen at any time of the year.

Look during holidays. You may think that summer is a bad time to look for a job because people are on vacation. If you decide to wait until September, when everyone is back at work, that may be a big mistake. Some job experts claim that summer is one of the best times to look, because there is less competition. They say that Christmas time is even better, since not many people are looking then. And offices can be a bit more relaxed and people are in a better mood during the holidays.

You've already done some of the preliminary work. You've taught yourself how to create a positive mindset. You've made sure that your online image is acceptable and won't cause you any trouble. You've chosen a professional email address and an appealing voice-mail message. You've created an effective elevator pitch that tells the world in 15 to 30 seconds who you are and what you can do.

Now it's time to get serious and begin the heavy work.

Preparing your resume

The first thing you need to do is to write a resume. For some people, this is one of the most difficult steps, but for most jobs having an effective resume is crucial. Creating a resume will also help you map out the direction you want to take your job search. You will also want to consider putting together a JIST card, which is discussed later in this chapter.

A resume provides a summary of your skills and experience and lets potential employers know what you can do to contribute to their company. It will help you figure out what skills and experience you have and which of them are appropriate for a particular job. It may also help you determine the types of jobs you might be able to do, if you don't know already.

Include nonpaid experience to cover gaps in employment. If you haven't had many jobs, be creative and include your experience, even if it was nonpaid or volunteer. For example, if you cared for an older relative, you can say "elder care, private home." You can even include the work you did in prison. Maybe you performed janitorial or kitchen duties. Some prisons have furniture making or other shops, and you can put that experience on your resume as well. You can put the job title of the job you did while incarcerated and the dates you were employed. You probably will want to put that you worked for the State of California, or wherever you were incarcerated, rather than San Quentin or another prison.

This type of experience will cover "gaps in time" on your resume. Most employers don't like to see gaps in time, because they have no idea what you were doing during those periods.

Types of resumes

There are two basic types of resumes—chronological and functional—and a third type that combines both of them.

Chronological resume. A chronological resume lists the jobs you have had in the order you have had them. It includes the job title, the company and location where you worked, the dates you worked there and the duties of the job, with your most recent employment at the top.

Functional resume. A functional resume is quite different. It lists your skills and then describes under each skill what you have done in various jobs that uses that skill.

Many employers prefer the chronological resume, because it is straightforward and shows exactly what people have done in the exact order they have done it in. It also blatantly highlights gaps in employment and focuses on job titles and companies rather than skills.

Combination resume. A combination functional/chronological resume does both and is the best choice if you have gaps in your employment history, which most ex-offenders do. It is also a good thing to use if you are looking for a job that is different than those you have had in the past. With a functional resume you can highlight the skills that may be transferred to a new type of job requiring similar skills and talents.

For example, you may have worked in a retail store serving customers but would like to get into the hospitality industry, maybe as a front-desk clerk in a hotel. The customer service skills you developed in a store are the same type of skills that you would use working in a hotel. So in a functional resume you would focus on those skills.

Or maybe you drove a truck but would like to work as a forklift operator in a warehouse. Again, many of your skills are transferable. In a combination functional/chronological resume you would list your skills and how you used them in one section, followed by your job history, with the names of the companies you worked for, the title(s) you held and the dates you worked there.

You can see examples of resumes in Appendix C.

Devote time. Set aside an afternoon to begin work on your resume. List every job you've ever had, the names of the companies you worked for, their addresses, and your bosses' names and contact info. If any of these companies no longer exist, you should try to find out where your former bosses are and how to get in touch with them.

Then write down all of the skills you used or developed in those jobs. If you have access to a computer, you can search for sample resumes of the jobs you've had to get ideas of what skills to include. You can also look at job ads on websites such as Craigslist to see exactly what qualifications employers are looking for.

Examples of two jobs and the skills they require:

Restaurant server

Good interpersonal, verbal and written communication skills
Service orientation
Able to work in fast-paced environment
Culinary knowledge
Pleasant attitude
Professional appearance
Good organizational skills
Strong attention to detail
Energetic and enthusiastic

Carpenter's assistant

Knowledge of residential construction
Ability to use basic hand tools
Skill in reading blueprints
Good interpersonal relationship skills
Ability to follow directions
Good listening skills
Attention to detail
Organization skills
Valid driver's license

If you've forgotten where you worked

If you've had a lot of jobs or haven't worked for a while, it's possible you may have forgotten where you've worked. If that happens, the best thing you can do is to fill out a Social Security Administration form SSA-750, which you can find and download by searching online.

You must fill out the form with your name, birth date and social security number and say why you need the information. You'll have to pay a fee, which ranges from $15 for one year's record to $35 for 10 years and more if you need information from a longer time period.

You send the form in with your payment and will receive a detailed report with the names and addresses of your former employers during the years you requested and the amount of time you worked for them, as well as how much you earned.

Writing your resume

Once you have a list of the jobs you've done and the skills and personality traits related to those jobs, you're ready to a write a resume and cover letter.

If you want to create a resume on your own, you will find help putting it together on the Internet. Microsoft.com has some excellent resume and cover letter templates to use for free.

For more tips, search online for "how to write a resume" and "how to write a cover letter." On some of the sites that come up you will find resume builders that will help you create your resume. Just type in the information, and they will do some of the work for you. Job search expert and author Susan Ireland has step-by-step advice on writing resumes on her website: www.susanireland.com/resume/how-to-write.

A faster and even better way to learn how to write a resume is to Google the title of the job you want to do followed by "resume," for example "carpenter's assistant resume." This will turn up examples of other people's resumes that you can get ideas from. Don't copy them, though, because employers may be searching the Internet to see what kinds of resumes they can find there, too.

Highlight strengths. When you actually do sit down to write your resume, make sure you think about what skills, attitudes and desires you possess that fit the type of job you're interested in. These are your strengths. Emphasize those strengths with bullet points in your resume to make them stand out. Always think about the employer and the company's needs, and ask yourself how you can meet those needs with your skills.

Include quotes. There's another thing you can do. Very few people do this, but it will set you apart from the others. And that's exactly what you want to do. This is to include quotes from customers, vendors, past employers or even from people who worked with you when you did volunteer work or other activities. These quotes will tell people how you performed a job well, how reliable you are or how easy you are to work with. Include these quotes as bullet points under the particular job they are related to.

Use PAR stories. Wherever you can in the jobs that you list on your resume, try to include PAR stories. PAR stands for problem, approach, resolution. In other words, you state a problem you encountered in a job, tell what approach you took to solve it, and explain how that fixed the problem in the end. These stories give employers a concrete idea of what you can accomplish.

In addition to including these PAR stories in your resume, you will want to memorize and practice telling them. Practice either just to yourself out loud or maybe to a friend or family member. PARs are a great way to give employers an idea of your accomplishments. They will also often come in handy when the hiring manager says during the interview, "*Tell me about a time when ...*" You can use a PAR story to tell them how you handled that certain situation.

Keep in mind that a resume is a marketing tool rather than a history of every job you have ever had and every duty you have ever performed. Stick with the important points and stress things that will make you look competent and capable of doing the job that you're applying for.

If you're bilingual, mention it. If you're bilingual, especially if you speak fluent Spanish, be sure to include that fact in your resume. Hispanics are the fastest growing ethnic group in the U.S. and now make up 16 percent of this nation's population. More and more businesses—whether they are service providers, retail stores, restaurants or offices—are interested in reaching the Hispanic market, and being able to speak Spanish may give you an advantage for some jobs.

Get help. If you haven't had much experience with resumes before, the best way to create one may be to visit your local American Job Center. These centers were mentioned in the previous chapter. They have job counselors who can help you put together your resume or give you suggestions on how to improve what you already have. Their services are free.

One thing to keep in mind is that the resume must fit the job you are applying for. Many people prepare a separate resume for each job, targeted to that particular job. You should use some of the same words that are in the job description, if there is one, to describe your experience. That way what you say you have done closely matches what the employer is looking for. You need to remember that the hiring managers are not trying to find the ten best resumes. Rather they are trying to weed out the 90 that they don't want to consider.

Posting your resume

Be sure to post your resume on websites like LinkedIn and Monster.com. This is a tactic used by white-collar employees and often overlooked by blue-collar or hourly workers. No matter what type of job you are looking for, you definitely want to do this. Since few blue-collar or hourly workers post their resumes on websites, doing so will help you stand out and get noticed by potential employers. If they search these sites for candidates doing your type of work, you will be one of the few they will find.

When a resume might not work

The resume is your sales tool, but what if you don't have much to sell? What if you've been incarcerated for months or years and have big gaps in employment? Or what if the jobs you've had were only for a very short period of time?

Employers don't like gaps in employment, and they like stable employees. So what do you do?

In this case, a resume might work against you. Instead of sending out a resume, you'll have to rely more on your network and other resources to build a relationship with someone who might be able to hire you.

You can say, *"I'm working on my resume now. Would you mind if I bring it to the interview?"* All resumes look better when delivered in person. Some employment experts believe that you should never send a resume ahead of time but should leave it behind after the interview.

If you need to send something, send a well-crafted letter and a JIST card, which is explained later in this chapter, instead of a resume. Your letter should summarize everything that a longer resume would cover. Tell the hiring manager how you found out about the job, what your qualifications are and why you would be an excellent person for the position.

Creating a cover letter

Never send a resume without a cover letter. A cover letter gives you a chance to highlight your experience in a paragraph or two or with a series of bullet points. It is more personal than a resume and lets you tell potential employers why they should hire you.

You should tailor the cover letter to each specific job description and company. Obtaining a bit of knowledge about the firm helps to customize the cover letter, focusing on what you can do for the company if you are hired, rather than just focusing on your past performance. Some employers read the cover letter first, and if they're not impressed won't even look at the resume.

Make sure that you personalize your cover letter, telling the hiring manager why you are a good fit for that particular job. If you know the hiring manager's name, include it. If you don't, you can write "Dear (company name or department) Hiring Manager."

To get a better idea of how to write a cover letter, search online for "cover letters" or visit your local American Job Center, where a job counselor can help you do this. Job search expert and author Susan Ireland has some good examples of cover letters on her website: www.susanireland.com/letter/cover-letter-examples.

Putting together a master application

At the same time that you're putting together your resume, you should use that same information to create a master application form. This document will have all of the details about the schools—high school or GED and beyond—you've attended, the jobs you've held and the places you've volunteered. The form will also include the contact information for your references. It's important to have one of these so when you fill out a job application, either at an interview or online, you will have all the information you need right there.

You can download a master application form online at http://bas.berkeley.net/jobsearch.html.

Creating a JIST card

One thing that will really set you apart and work in your favor is to make a JIST card. JIST stands for *Job Information Seeking and Training* and was coined by the late Michael Farr, a career expert and author, who came up with the idea of the JIST card, which is like a mini-resume.

This card, usually 3″ x 5″ but can be any size, is a brief summary of a person and what they can do. It includes the person's name, contact info, position desired, a list of their skills and three words that describe their personality.

These cards can be given out to friends, acquaintances, people you meet and everyone in your "circle of contacts" (discussed in Step 4). They can be enclosed with thank-you notes or sent with a cover letter instead of a resume. The beauty of a JIST card is that not only is it unique, but it includes nothing that can be perceived as negative such as gaps in employment. You can see an example and how to create it in Appendix D.

Dealing with your record

Throughout your job search you're going to have to deal with your record, so you'd better prepare for the inevitable from the beginning.

Background check. First of all, it's important to know exactly what's in your record and what people can find out about you. There are companies that do background checks for a fee that will tell you what information can be found. It doesn't cost a whole lot of money and is probably well worth it. Almost all employers do background checks these days, and they will find out your record, so it's better to deal with it first in your own way. You'll learn how to do that in Step 5.

RAP sheet. You can get your RAP—Record of Arrest and Prosecution—sheet from the state government where you live. (California residents can find step-by-step instructions on how to do this in Appendix H.) You should only be concerned if you have been convicted, however. In California and some other states, it's illegal for employers to ask if you were arrested. They can only ask if you were convicted. If you live in another state, check out the law for that state.

Once you know exactly what your record is and if it does include a conviction, you may be able to expunge or get rid of the conviction, especially if it was only a misdemeanor (see Appendix H). But that can take a long time, and you can't let it stop you from your job search.

The turnaround packet

Ultimately you want to turn your life experiences, including your incarceration, into strengths and a reason for the hiring manager to offer you a job. That is why you should put together what Larry Robbin, a nationally known expert in the area of workforce development, calls a "turnaround packet."

This packet is a set of documents that you will show to the hiring managers during interviews. It includes information you put together that is intended to turn the potential employer's perception of you around and realize you would make a good employee. Its purpose is to let them know that you have overcome the adversity that put you in jail or prison and that you are ready to be a productive worker. You want to convince the hiring manager that the person you were when you committed the crime is not the person you are today. Your turnaround packet demonstrates that and clearly shows you have been rehabilitated.

Be sure to only include items that emphasize the fact that you have been rehabilitated and not draw attention to areas that still need work. The items you should include are listed in Appendix J.

Putting together a turnaround packet can be a lot of work, but your potential employer is sure to be impressed that you took the time and effort to do so. It's also a very organized way to state what you've done to improve your life and gives you a lot of positive things to talk about in your interview.

You will take this turnaround packet to interviews and also prepare a turnaround talk, which you will learn how to do in Step 5. In both cases, it's best for you to refer to yourself as a person in reentry and not an ex-offender.

Creating a list of potential employers

Once you have your resume and turnaround packet together and have a good idea of what you're looking for, it's time to create a list of potential employers.

One hundred employers. This is a crucial step in the process, so take it very seriously. Set aside a day or two to put together a list of 100 potential employers. It doesn't matter whether these employers have advertised job openings or not, since most jobs aren't advertised anyway. The goal is to try to contact as many companies as possible and get on their radar. They may have immediate needs, or when a job does open up in the future, they might contact you about it.

When you're making the list don't just go after big companies. That would be a huge mistake. It's the smaller employers who create most of the jobs in this country. Smaller employers, those with fewer than 250 people, hire nearly 75 percent of all workers in the U.S. So don't ignore them. In fact, depending on what type of work you do, it might be best to concentrate on small companies. Your odds at finding a job would probably be better.

Create boundaries. First decide which industry you wish to work in and what size of company you prefer to work for. Then create the physical boundaries of the area in which you would like to work. For example, you may only want to consider companies within 30 miles of where you live.

Search online databases. After you have created the boundaries, it's time to figure out 100 companies that meet your specifications. You can do this in several ways. A very effective way is to check out the American Job Center's employer locator, which can be found at www.careerinfonet.org/employerlocator. You can search this database by industry, location or occupation. It will pull up all the companies in a certain area that match your criteria and give you the name of each company and its address, telephone number and approximate number of employees.

You can also search in www.whitepages.com, an online telephone directory. Enter a type of business and location, and it will display all of the businesses of that type in the area in a listing that includes their addresses and phone numbers. These can be copied and pasted onto a Word document to create a list to work from. If you don't have access to a computer, you can find companies by using the local telephone Yellow Pages or by going to the library or an American Job Center and using their computers.

Another place to look is www.linkedin.com, which is like Facebook for business, but you have to open an account first. Make sure to open a free account, because you have to pay for a premium account. Once you open an account, go in and click "companies" on the bar across the top of the home page. Then click on the blue "search" button on the left column of the next page. You can choose "industries." This function brings up companies all over the world in those industries, but if you put in a specific city, it will only call up companies in that area. You can further refine the search by selecting the size of a company in terms of number of employees.

When you are putting together your list, make sure to think in terms of which companies would have the type of jobs that you qualify for. Otherwise you're wasting your time.

Check rating sites. Another way to build your list is by looking at rating sites, such as Yelp (www.yelp.com), Diamond Certified (www.diamondcertified.org),

Home Advisor (www.homeadvisor.com) and Houzz (www.houzz.com). These websites offer reviews of various businesses, so you can get a better idea of the products and services they offer. Go into any of them and search by location and business type.

Many people in reentry have found restaurants to be ex-offender friendly, and Yelp is a great place to learn about restaurants and what people think of them. You can get an idea of the food they serve and the quality of their service by reading Yelp reviews. Servers in some Bay Area restaurants are known to make $100 to $300 per day in tips. According to the *Wall Street Journal*, at high-end dinner houses head waiters can make $80,000 to $150,000 per year, including tips.

Look for the businesses in your area that have many reviews, which means they're popular. Print out a map of the area on Google Maps and put an "X" on the locations of businesses that look worth visiting. Develop a list of at least 10 restaurants and approach them all in a day, if you can. Be sure to go between 2:00 p.m. and 4:00 p.m., however, so you won't interrupt a busy lunch or dinner service. The manager is more likely to be available during those hours as well. Get in your car, catch public transportation or walk, with your cover letters and resumes or JIST cards in hand. You should also have your master application, just in case you're asked to fill out an application on the spot. Going to place after place after place will maximize your chances of getting hired.

Ask for the manager and tell them you've been reading their excellent reviews on Yelp and are impressed. That you'd be interested in finding out more about the business and how you can make a contribution. Make sure you take notes after you've visited each place, so you can email a letter thanking the hiring manager for meeting with you and reminding them of your qualifications and why you would be a good employee. You should include a JIST card as an attachment or imbedded in the email.

You should make at least 100 new contacts a month. You can do that by making phone calls, sending emails or showing up at a company's door. It's kind of like being a sales rep—making cold calls to find new business. In your case you're making cold calls to find a new job. And remember it's a numbers game. The more places you contact, the better your chances of finding a job.

If you're interested in nonprofits

Nonprofits can be open to giving people a second chance, and they might be a good source of potential job possibilities. Your compelling story may actually go further with a hiring manager at a nonprofit.

Start with Guide Star (www.guidestar.org), an organization that serves as an information clearinghouse for nonprofit organizations. It has just about everything you need to know about the organizations, including their goals, membership numbers and funding sources. After opening a complimentary account, you can search by keyword, organization name, and city, county or state to find out the nonprofits in a certain area. Within each listing, you can click on the organization's 990 form, which brings up its tax returns, and you can see the names of the key personnel, which can be helpful in determining who to talk to.

What makes a good job?

Positive answers to the following questions will contribute far more to job satisfaction than how "cool" a particular job seems to be. Use this checklist during your job search when you are contemplating whether or not to accept a job.

- Is the work moderately challenging?
- Does it require abilities that you enjoy using? Will you be working with words? Working with your hands? Working with details? Do you like being your own boss?
- Are there good co-workers?
- Is the boss easy to work with?
- Is the work environment pleasant?
- Is it an organization that you believe in? Is it an ethical company? Does it make a good product?
- Does it offer opportunities for you to keep learning? Is the job manageable and not too difficult but at the same time offer growth?
- Does it offer job security?
- Does it offer good enough pay? The pay should not be the overriding factor in your decision-making process, however. After taxes, the difference in income usually doesn't matter enough to make money the dominant factor.
- Does it offer good benefits? Particularly health care?
- Is the commute reasonable? If it's too long, you may get quickly burned out.

Thanks to Marty Nemko, career coach and author of *Cool Careers For Dummies*, for his research and ideas.

STEP 3

Accelerating the search: keeping the pace without crashing

"Nothing in this world can take the place of persistence. Talent will not; nothing is more common than unsuccessful people with talent. Genius will not; unrewarded genius is almost a proverb. Education will not; the world is full of educated derelicts. Persistence and determination alone are omnipotent. The slogan "press on" has solved and always will solve the problems of the human race."

– Calvin Coolidge, 30th President of the United States of America

Looking for a job is your job right now—your full-time job. And you need to devote most of your energy to the task. The technique you develop to search for a job is the most important step you will take in the process. So put a lot of time and effort into creating an effective technique, of which your attitude and efforts are the most important things.

Preparing for your job search

Before you can begin to look for a job, you need to do a few additional important things to get ready.

Set aside a place to work. This could be an "office" if you have a spare room in your house or apartment. Or it could be a desk in the corner of your living room. Or it could even be your kitchen table. Conducting a serious job search will be difficult if you don't have a physical place to do it. A library or a coffee shop, however, can also serve as your "office." Many entrepreneurs who work out of their homes spend hours each day at their local coffee shop. You can see them busily tapping away at their laptop keyboards in just about any coffee shop you go to.

Whatever your workspace turns out to be, the important thing to remember is that when you sit down at this place, you must be ready to work.

A telephone is essential. In fact, it will be your most important job search tool. As you will learn when reading this book, contacting potential employers by phone or in person is the most effective way to find a job.

Create a proper mindset. Set aside a start time, maybe 8:30 in the morning, and get to work. Some people say it helps to dress up just as if you were going to work, since that's exactly what you are doing. Others prefer to just wear jeans and a sweatshirt. Some even work in their pajamas, but that's not a good idea. Whatever helps you to get in the proper mindset to look for a job is what should be done.

Since looking for a job is a full-time job, you should plan to work seven or eight hours a day on your search. It takes a lot of effort to find a job. Some people say it's much harder to find a job than to actually do the job once you get it.

Make sure you do everything you can—a zillion things—in the first week, because that will set the pace and help you keep your motivation and momentum up in the weeks to come. Even one job lead at the beginning can make all the difference in keeping you going.

Be realistic. Many people are attracted to glamorous jobs or what they would consider cool careers. These jobs might be working as an actor, a news anchor, a filmmaker, a fashion model, a winery worker or whatever else is hip and fashionable. The problem with these cool jobs is that there is way too much competition for them, and at least on the bottom rungs, the pay can be fairly pathetic, since people will accept low salaries just to get into the business.

Be realistic and realize that any job you like to do can be rewarding. There are many factors to consider when choosing a job, although there are some things you won't be able to find out until after you actually start the work.

What to consider. Important aspects to consider include, most importantly, whether the tasks you will be performing are things you really enjoy doing. You should also try to figure out whether the job will be challenging enough, without being so difficult that it will constantly stress you out. Among other things to consider are the work environment, the personalities of the co-workers and the boss, the pay, the benefits, the commute, job security and whether the company and its products are something you can be proud of.

Avoid procrastination

Procrastination is the worst enemy of a job seeker. It can prevent you from getting a job and is the one thing you absolutely must learn how to manage.

There are many reasons why people procrastinate. Just pick one. Some people procrastinate because they fear success. Others do it because they fear failure. Still others are perfectionists and don't want to tackle a project, because they're afraid they won't be able to do it well enough.

Make it fun. You can no doubt think of many things more fun than looking for a job, but try to make your job search as enjoyable as possible. Look at it like a game or a shopping trip. You're shopping for a job. Think of all the people you'll meet and what you'll learn in the process. The goal is to find a job that is a good fit. Of course you have to find an employer to hire you, but you also want to be in a place where you will be happy. After all, you're going to spend between 35 and 40 hours a week there, and that's a lot of time to be miserable.

In order to manage your procrastination, you must focus on the task at hand. Think about what you need to do to get one step further in your job search, even if it's just a baby step. Decide what can be accomplished during the next hour, and do it.

Marty Nemko, career coach and author of *Cool Careers For Dummies*, offers some other useful information about dealing with procrastination.

One thing he says is that you have to accept being uncomfortable. To be successful it is essential to occasionally do tasks that are difficult and aren't as much fun as other things.

Also, believe that you can survive failure. Yes, you will sometimes fail, but if you don't try something out, you will never succeed either. Even if you keep getting rejections, which you will, you're moving your job search forward just by getting out there and doing it. If you keep at it, ultimately you will find a job.

Look at yourself as being able to follow-through on what you attempt. You may want to say to yourself, *"I am a follow-through person."* Say it enough, and you just may become one.

One-minute task. If what you're doing seems overwhelming, divide it into smaller steps. Write them down and as you do each of them, you'll accomplish the larger task. Another approach is to try to do just one thing, what Nemko calls a one-minute task. He also talks about a one-minute struggle. If you get to something difficult, just spend one minute on it. If you can't do it in one minute, do it differently or get help.

Find a way to make what you're doing more fun. Work to music. Make it a game and see how many things you can get done in an afternoon.

Perhaps most importantly of all, stay focused. Get other things out of your mind. Don't be distracted. And stay positive. The more you think or talk about negative things, the more real they become. The neurons in your brain become stronger, and it becomes harder to counterattack negative thoughts. The important thing is to do something, no matter how small. Behavior change usually comes before attitude change, so if you alter what you are doing, the way you think about the situation will be different as a result.

Create your own luck

Certain people seem to be lucky. They always get the breaks, success comes easy to them, and they sail through life. But does luck really exist—outside of things like winning the lottery—or do lucky people do things to achieve their goals that other people don't?

There are, in fact, actions to take that will make you seem lucky. You can set yourself up to be in the pathway of success. First just do something. And if that doesn't work, do something else. Be persistent. Call your list of companies.

Make sure all your friends and acquaintances know you're looking for a job and what kind of work you can do. When the right job just happens to open up, it may be your hard work, rather than luck, that made it happen.

Put together a to-do list

The first thing to do every morning is to create a to-do list for the day. You can also do it the night before, but if you do it ahead of time, reexamine your list and make any changes you feel necessary, just in case you had some new ideas in the meantime.

Some of the items on the list may be things you didn't have time to complete the day before. Others may be brand-new. Put the most difficult tasks at the top of the list, and do those first. It's amazing how good you will feel if you get the hard things out of the way. Then the rest of the day will be easier, and you'll save time and stress not worrying about the tough stuff. Creating a to-do list helps you focus on what needs to get done. It also makes you accountable—if nothing else, accountable to yourself.

As you complete each task, cross it off the list. That will make you feel like you have accomplished something—or many things—that hour or that morning or that day.

Plan to give yourself a reward if you get everything that you planned to do done. Take a walk, call a friend to chat, eat a bowl of ice cream—whatever you enjoy doing that is legal and doesn't take too much time, cost too much money or cause anyone any harm.

Plan ahead. Look ahead and schedule tasks for the future. Maybe you have an interview in a few days and have certain things, such as researching the company, to accomplish before that. Put that task on your schedule for a day or so before the interview. Go to an office supply store and buy a daily, weekly or monthly planner. These spiral-ring calendars provide a great way to help you keep on track.

They cost about $8 to $15, but if you can't afford one, you can sometimes get free planner-type calendars from businesses, which give them away for advertising.

These are a bit hard to find, but many businesses give away wall calendars—the type with a page for each month—so you can also use these, although they're not quite as good as a planner. Another no-cost possibility is to print a calendar off the Internet. There are many templates available online. Just Google "blank calendar," and you'll find them.

Sometimes what you have to do may seem scary or too much to handle, but when you actually perform the task, it's often not as bad as you thought it would be. In fact, it might be surprisingly pleasant.

Set deadlines. If you do have trouble getting going on something that needs to be done, set a deadline. Tell yourself that within the next hour, you have to call 10 people, write a rough draft of your cover letter, or whatever. Set a timer to keep on track. The digital timers used for cooking are great, because they tell you exactly how many minutes remain.

If you continue to have trouble with procrastination, keep a procrastination log. Use a small notebook. Every time you decide to put off doing something, write it down. Write down how you feel about doing it and why you decided to do it later. This will not only help you realize why you're procrastinating but will also help hold you accountable. When you really analyze why things are being put off, you will realize that there is no acceptable reason not to do them.

Create a vision poster

You should also visualize the benefits to be gained by getting a job. I have a friend who is an expert at that. She was looking for work and put a big piece of poster board on the wall in front of her computer. On the poster board she pasted pictures cut out from magazines. These pictures were symbols of her goals—what type of work she wanted, how much money she wanted to make, and all the things she would be able to do with that money.

She cut out pictures of a nice-looking house; a waterfall in Hawaii, where she likes to go on vacation; a German shepherd like her dog, Eve; a Jeep Cherokee, her favorite car; even a hot fudge sundae, her favorite dessert. Every day she would start out by looking at the poster and all the things she would get if she found her dream job. This type of poster is not only fun to make, but it also will inspire you to meet your goals.

Don't break the chain

When Jerry Seinfeld was starting his career as a comic, he developed a very effective technique to help him keep good work habits. He called it "don't break the chain."

Seinfeld believed that to be better at his job, he had to write better jokes, and the way to write better jokes was to write them every day. He took a big calendar with an entire year on one page and hung it on his wall. Every day when he wrote jokes, he put a big red X on that day on the calendar and after a few days had a chain with all the Xs linked together. If he decided not to work one day, he wouldn't be able to put in an X on the calendar for that day and would break the chain. The goal is to not break the chain. Take your job search one day at a time, and never stop. Don't break the chain.

Different ways to look for work

Now that you've decided to devote each and every day to your job search, the real work begins. There are several ways to look for a job, and they are all effective to a certain degree. The key, however, is to not just choose one of these methods. Ideally, you should use them all. *The two most effective job search methods, however, are to develop your network and to contact potential employers directly*, so pay very careful attention to how to do these things, which are explained later in this section and also in Appendix A.

Google is your best friend. Anything you want to know about your job search can probably be found on the Internet. Use search words related to what you want to find out. To be even more specific, you can use Google's advanced search. Click on the "advanced search" icon on the Google home page and set whatever parameters you would like.

Internet job boards. Just about everyone begins job hunting by looking at advertisements. In the past these ads were only in newspapers, but not many companies advertise in newspapers anymore, so they're not the best place to look.

Most companies now use the Internet to publicize their job openings, and there are many job sites to explore. The most popular site for most employers is Craigslist.org, an online marketplace where people can sell things and provide information to people. Job listings are an important part of this. There are Craigslist postings for most major cities, and hundreds of jobs of all types, from laborers and forklift operators to directors of marketing and nonprofit executives.

Other job boards include Monster.com and Careerbuilder.com. For government jobs, there's USAjobs.gov, and for high-tech jobs, Dice.com. Companies pay a fee to list their job openings on these sites, but job seekers can look at them for free.

Aggregator websites. There are three other excellent sites—Indeed.com, Simplyhired.com and Linkup.com—that work a bit differently. These sites are called aggregators, which means they pull job listings from all kinds of other sites. They have some listings from the sites listed above (but not Craigslist), along with job openings from various company websites. Each is keyword and ZIP code searchable and you can sign up for job alerts just as you can with other Internet job boards.

All of the online job boards mentioned here are not only very popular with employers but with job seekers as well. Many job postings will bring in hundreds of resumes, so unless your background is exceptionally suited to the position being advertised, you probably won't hear from the employer.

Don't be like some people and use this method as your main job-seeking tactic. If you do, you'll spend a lot of time sitting around waiting for employers to call you. You have better things to do than that. But also don't ignore these job boards. Instead of looking at them every day, spend three or four hours searching them once a week, except maybe Craigslist, which you can look at every day or two, since it has the most listings.

Company and organization websites. Company and organization websites are other places to look. Although Indeed.com, Simplyhired.com and

Linkup.com pulls job listings from corporate websites, they only pull from certain companies. If you're very interested in a handful of companies or organizations, you should check their websites once a week or so to see if they have any jobs listed.

Some smaller companies may not have websites, or even if they do, they might not list their job openings on them. If you're interested in working at a small company, the best thing is to get to know people who can introduce you to the hiring manager, who is likely to be the owner.

If you're thinking about working for a nonprofit organization, check out Idealist.org and Opportunityknocks.org. As we mentioned in Step 2, nonprofits may be a good choice, since they are often more willing than other places to hire those in reentry.

Employment agencies

In the past, visiting an employment agency was one of the best ways to find a job. This is not really true anymore, because employment agencies charge hefty fees. Some companies, however, still use employment agencies, and these agencies often have temporary divisions, which hire workers for periods of one day to several months or even a year or more. You will learn more about these in Step 4.

Government jobs

Government jobs are available at both the local, state and federal level and offer an exceptional number of opportunities for all types of employment, ranging from entry-level labor and clerical jobs to professional positions.

Government jobs sometimes pay higher rates than those in the private sector and also provide excellent benefits, including pensions, which are becoming more and more unusual these days. Government jobs are usually very stable, although some states suffering financial crises, may on occasion cut back their employees' salaries and hours. The term they use is furlough, which means employees work a day or two less per month and get their salaries cut accordingly.

Federal government jobs. The federal government employs about 2.7 million people, 84 percent of whom are outside of the Washington, D.C. area. Previously the federal government job application process was very time consuming and complicated, but it has been simplified to make it easier for people to apply.

The federal government includes agencies such as the National Park Service, the U.S. Postal Service and countless others, which all have job openings at various locations across the country. You can find out about specific openings at USAjobs.gov, which has a database of jobs that can be searched by keywords and by city, state or ZIP code. At DCjobsource.com/fed.html you will find a list of links to federal agencies, most of which have jobs listed on their websites.

California state government jobs. The place to look for California state government jobs is at Jobs.ca.gov. The site's database is searchable by county, keywords and other criteria. The state of California has even better benefits than the federal government and offers an especially good retirement pension.

Another website to check out, calopps.org, is where California's cities and public agencies list their job openings.

Part-time work

You may want to look at part-time work, because part-time jobs are usually not as competitive as full-time positions. In the beginning, it might be necessary to piece together two or three part-time jobs to make enough money to survive. Hopefully one of the companies you are doing part-time work for will like you enough that when a full-time position opens up, they will offer it to you.

It's a good idea to take an easier-to-get job (stepping-stone or launch-pad job) even if you believe that you are overqualified for the position. An object in motion tends to stay in motion. There are many success stories out there of people taking a couple of stepping-stone jobs and then going on to find excellent full-time work.

Some part-time jobs even come with benefits. Safeway, Peet's Coffee & Tea and Starbucks offer benefits to part-time workers. Get creative. Want to stay out of prison or jail? Get a job! You will sentence yourself to a life of poverty unless you find one.

Craigslist gigs. You can check the Gigs section of Craigslist to find such short-term jobs as yard work, labor, gardening, bartending and serving, plumbing or handyman work. Although these are short-term jobs, they can occasionally lead to more work.

Petition signature collecting. Another possible part-time job is as a petition signature collector. These are the folks who stand outside of grocery stores and other places and solicit signatures on behalf of a cause or ballot initiative. Not only can the hiring process be quicker and money not too difficult, it may present opportunities to network with the public and find other job leads.

In order to be qualified in the state of California, you must be a U.S. citizen, a California resident, at least 18 years of age and not currently on parole. Probation is okay. For qualifications in other states, check with your secretary of state's office.

To find a job as a petition signature collector, check Craigslist and search on Google for "petitioners (insert city of interest) paid." You may need to experiment with search combinations for the best results. A variety of jobs should appear. Some with hourly pay, plus incentive pay for each signature. Part-time and full-time opportunities usually exist that claim one can earn between $10 and $40 per hour.

Ask for leads

Talk to everyone you know, and tell them you are looking for a job and what kind of job you would like to do. Talk to relatives. Talk to friends. Talk to neighbors. Talk to people in the community. Maybe you're a regular customer at a hardware store or a local restaurant. Tell the owner what you're doing. They come into contact with a lot of people and may hear of something. You can get more details about who to contact in Appendix M, which includes Larry Robbin's Circle of Contacts.

Hidden job market

The best way to get a job, especially in tough economic times when the competition is fierce, is through someone you know. Through your contacts you will be able to tap into what is called the hidden job market. The hidden job market is full of jobs that are not advertised in the newspaper or on Internet job boards.

Some employers don't want to wade through the hundreds of resumes they would receive from postings on Internet job boards, so they use their employees, friends and contacts to help them find people to fill the open positions at their company. That way, potential employees also come referred, meaning that someone knows the job candidate and can vouch for them.

Pick up the phone

As you already know, the telephone is your most important job search tool. It's even more important than a computer, because the phone is the way you will be able to make a personal contact and more effectively get in touch with the people you need to talk to.

In fact, many job experts say that more than 80 percent of all jobs are unadvertised, and you can be sure that there is less competition for unadvertised jobs, since fewer people know about them. Calling people is known as the direct contact method, and it can be the most powerful way to get a job.

If at all possible try to get an interview without sending in a resume. Talk to the hiring manager—not someone in human resources or personnel but the person who is in charge of the department where you would like to work—and ask to be interviewed. If there are no jobs at the time when you call, tell them that you would like to get together to discuss future opportunities anyway.

By doing this, you might be able to find out about a job before it's advertised. There may not be anything available on the day you go into the company, but it's possible there's a job on the horizon. And you may be the first to know about it. And if they like you, they might hire you without interviewing anyone else.

Getting to the hiring manager. Picking up the phone is usually the easiest way to get the hiring manager's name. Say to the person who answers, *"I am trying to find out the name of the person who hires in (department). I want to send them a letter. How do you spell their last name? What is their official title?"* If they are not sure, ask if they have a company directory handy and can look it up.

Wrong extensions can often help direct you to the right person. Dial extensions starting with 1 or 2 and ask who is the hiring manager for whatever department you'd like to work in.

Avoid human resource departments. They support hiring managers during the selection process but don't typically decide who gets hired. Their primary purpose is to screen you out. Spend your time with the person who has the power to offer you a job—the hiring manager.

Instead of putting too much energy into polishing your resume or researching companies, spend most of your time finding the names of hiring managers to call.

Many job seekers are terrified to pick up the phone and call someone they don't know. But they shouldn't be. If you approach the calls in a persistent and professional manner, people will usually be very courteous in return. Projecting confidence whether real or pretend—faking it until you make it—is also an important component of an effective call. You may be afraid that you're imposing on people, but hiring managers are often looking for people. If you're convinced that you are a good worker and have what it takes to do the job, consider that you are doing them a favor.

Most people want to help others, and managers are often on the lookout for potential employees who will be a good fit for their department—if not for now, for sometime in the future. So don't be afraid. After making a few calls, it gets easier. You will get into a certain rhythm that will make you want to keep dialing.

Numbers game. Keep in mind that cold calling—picking up the phone and calling businesses you've never spoken to before—is a numbers game. The more people you contact, the greater chance you will have of getting someone who might be interested in calling you in for an interview. Be aware, however, that it could take as many as seven or eight times to get through to the right person.

You can also look at it like planting seeds. You're doing the groundwork—or planting the seeds—now that will develop into job opportunities later.

So pick up the phone and start calling in your most enthusiastic voice. You made your list of 100 companies or potential employers in Step 2. Now it's time to use it. Call 20 companies per day. Ask for the name of the hiring manager of the department or departments you are interested in. Talk to them about your abilities for the type of position you can do well. This is where you can use your 15-second elevator pitch and the information from your JIST card. Don't let the receptionist steer you to the human resources department. You must reach the hiring manager. Otherwise you're probably wasting your time.

Be enthusiastic and sincere. When talking on the phone, be sure to smile. That will come across. Some people also believe that you should stand up, because your voice will project better that way.

You also need to sound enthusiastic, whether on the phone or in person. Sound like you're really interested in finding out more about the company and its job possibilities. You may be nervous, but an enthusiastic voice will go a long way to convince a hiring manager to meet with you. Also be sincere in your interest. Enthusiasm and sincerity are two important qualities to exhibit, both during the job search and once you get a job.

Remember, it's important to give them a reason to want to take a look at your resume, interview you, or talk to you further. Just saying things like, *"I'm unemployed and can start work immediately,"* isn't going to get you in the door. Instead, focus on the company's needs and what you can do for the hiring manager.

Debra Angel McDougall and Elisabeth Harney Sanders-Park, authors of *The Six Reasons You'll Get the Job,* recommend giving hiring managers the top three reasons you would be an asset to the company. Make sure to let them know how you can help them. Don't ask if they're hiring. It's about their needs not yours.

For example, say something like, *"Hello Mr. Nelson, my name is Scott Jenkins. I have more than 10 years experience in ... (Refer to your JIST card and 15-second elevator pitch.) Could you use someone with my skills?"*

Call off-hours. If you really are too shy or nervous to call during office hours, or if you want to conduct a possibly faster and more efficient job search, call early in the morning or after the office closes, and use voice-mail.

Introduce yourself and leave a 15-second scripted message selling your strengths and telling the hiring manager that you are going to send an email (include your JIST card, since resumes are better to present in person) and want to get together. Although you should write out what you're going to say beforehand, don't make it sound like you're reading it.

Say *"I'd like to get together so I may elaborate more on my qualities and how I would be a good fit at (company name). I wonder if you would be kind enough to give me some advice on where I might turn to find job openings."* Remember if they have a job opening they'll tell you. Your approach is more like you're asking for job search guidance and advice rather than just asking for a job.

Sending email

The best thing to do is to tell them in your voice-mail message that you will follow up with an email. This way you can reach out to the hiring manager two different ways, since some people prefer communicating by email. When you send this email be sure to attach a JIST card, which we explained in Step 2. A JIST card usually works better than a resume, unless your resume is a perfect fit for the company you're contacting and has no significant gaps in time between jobs.

If you don't hear back in a day or two, call again. This will show them you're pleasantly persistent and can follow through on tasks, which are both traits that would make you a good employee.

Make sure you get the email address that the hiring manager actually uses. First find out the name of the hiring manager, either online or by calling the company and asking the operator. Then say, *"By the way, what's that person's email address?"*

If you already have the manager's name, call and say that you want to email the hiring manager some information and need their email address. Be sure to use that person's first and last name, and don't refer to them as Mr. or Ms.

So-and-so. For example say Larry Smith rather than Mr. Smith. And when you talk to hiring managers, make sure to get their direct telephone number and email address if you don't have them already. That way it will be easier to contact them later.

Some experts believe that you should only email someone after establishing initial phone or face-to-face contact, but others think it's fine to send an email regardless. If referred to a hiring manger by someone or an organization, always put "Referred by: and the name of the person or organization" in the email subject line.

Call/email/call/call technique

There is a very effective technique known as the call/email/call/call technique, and you should use this on the list of 100 companies you put together, at least those on the list that you don't plan to visit in person. We first learned of this technique from Marty Nemko, career coach and author of *Cool Careers For Dummies.*

Here's how it works:

First call. Call hiring managers from your list after hours and leave a message on their voice mail. The reason that you should call them after hours is that you have more control over what you say. This also frees up your workday to concentrate on other aspects of your job search.

Introduce yourself and leave a 15-second scripted elevator pitch, as described in Step 1, selling your strengths and advising them that you will be sending them an email (be sure to include your JIST card) and want to get together. Although you should write out what you're going to say, don't make it sound like you're reading it. You can use your JIST card to create an effective phone script.

Say, for example, *"Hi I'm _______ and my phone number is ________. I love doing________ and I'm really good at it. I'm confident that I have the experience that could help your company succeed. I think I can offer you (give your three top assets)."*

"Again, my phone number is_____ (say it and then repeat it) I'd like to get together so I may elaborate more on my qualities and how I would be a good fit at (company name). I wonder if you would be kind enough to give me some information about working at your company. As soon as I get off the phone I'm going to follow up with an email, and I hope to hear from you soon."

Remember if they have a job opening they'll tell you. Your approach is more like you're asking for job search guidance and advice.

If you don't hear back. If you don't receive a call back from the hiring manager within two to three days, call during business hours.

Say, *"This is ______. My phone number is ____ (if voice-mail). I left a voice-mail message and sent you an email on ________, I know how things can slip through the cracks, so I'm following up. I'd appreciate getting together with you to find out more about working at your company and would like to know when you might be available for a short informational meeting. (If voice mail) Again, this is ______ and my number is _____. I look forward to hearing from you soon."*

If still no response. If you don't receive a call back from the hiring manager within a week, call one more time during business hours. This demonstrates confidence—even if you have to fake it—and shows that you are pleasantly persistent and able to follow-up.

Say, *"This is ______. My phone number is ____ (if voice-mail). I've left a couple of voice mail messages and know how things can slip through the cracks. I don't mean to be a pest but I hope you're the type who appreciates persistence. I just wanted to let you know that I think I can contribute to your company and would love to talk to you about it. I'd appreciate hearing back from you, but if I don't I promise not to call you another time. Again, this is ______ and my number is _____. I look forward to hearing from you soon."*

Don't be a pest. Well-directed, polite persistence is usually welcome. Even if you are angry or irritated about not being called back, keep it out of your voice, and continue to sound positive and enthusiastic.

Remember, employers are desperate for enthusiastic, self-directed employees. By using this method, you will be light-years ahead of the competition.

If this strategy does not work, however, it is usually for two reasons. Your target market is dead, and there aren't any jobs. Or your pitch may be dead; it is just not compelling. It's critical to sound enthusiastic. America is the land of enthusiasm—not irrational exuberance, but enthusiasm.

Be sure to keep a list of the people you called and the dates you called them, with notes about what they said if you were able to reach them.

Just walk in

Visit any potential employer, factory or office that interests you, even if they don't have any job openings. Be friendly to the receptionist or whomever else you meet when you enter. Tell them you'd like to talk to the hiring manager of the department you're interested in. It's probably best to call ahead and find out who that is, so you can ask for them by name. As mentioned before, avoid the human resources department, because you're usually wasting your time talking to them.

If you do get a chance to meet the hiring manager, ask them about working at the company. Tell them about your skills, and ask for their advice. If you make a good enough impression, you'll have an inside track. They may even be willing to create a job for you if they like you enough, but this is pretty unlikely. If nothing else, you've made contact with someone who may be able to help you find a job, either at their own company or through one of their contacts.

If the hiring manager is not in, ask to speak to someone else in the department. Have a brief chat—don't take more than five or six minutes, since they're probably busy—and get to know that person. Hopefully they will put in a good word about you with the hiring manager. When you contact the hiring manager, mention that you met with their colleague and are very interested in learning more about working at the company.

Since you've already made a positive contact, you could either email the hiring manager or go back to see them again. But don't go more than once a week. Going back shows reliability and persistence, the qualities employers are looking for. Don't be a pest, however. Be polite and apologize. Tell the receptionist or cashier something like, *"I'm sorry to bother you again, but I'd really like to see ______(hiring manager's name)."*

Retail jobs. If you'd like to get a job in retail, for example, pick a store you think you might like to work at and walk in on a day when business is slow. A good time might be 9:00 a.m. or 10:00 a.m. on a weekday morning, when there is not likely to be many customers. Ask for the manager. Deliver your elevator pitch and share with them that you like their business because—fill in the blank—and that you would love to work at their store. This is just an example for one type of business. The approach works just as well for others, say auto repair shops, warehouses, etc.

Restaurant work. If you're interested in working at a particular restaurant, have lunch there—it's cheaper than dinner—a few times, if you can afford it. Make sure to go later in the lunch period, maybe 1:30 or so, or when things begin to slow down. Get to know the wait staff, and after a few times, tell one of them that you would like to meet the hiring manager.

This technique takes a bit of courage, but if you put yourself on the line, you'll have a better chance of finding a job. Walk into 10 places per day—10 stores, 10 restaurants, 10 offices—and ask for the job! Go with your resume or JIST card and master application and most enthusiastic personality. If you keep doing this, you're going to get hired faster than if you just send in your resume. It is the unusual employer or hiring manager who does not appreciate diligence and persistence.

No phone calls

Many job listings on the Internet specifically say "no phone calls." You may want to take a bit of a risk and call anyway, however. On many job websites, "no phone calls" is just one of the restrictions that employers can choose. Call the company, find out who the hiring manager for the position is and try to talk to them. Begin by apologizing, saying you know that the ad said "no phone calls," but that you are so excited about the position that you just had to call. Then go on to talk about your qualifications and what you have to offer to the company.

Follow the 80/20 rule

It might be best to apply the 80/20 rule to your job search. Workforce development expert Larry Robbin has done research that indicates that 8 percent of employers will hire an ex-offender, 12 percent might hire one and 80 percent won't. Even if you were to be less optimistic and assume that 80 percent will say "no," and 20 percent will say "maybe," that's still 20 out of 100. Those odds are definitely worth pursuing, and your job is to find employers who will say "yes."

Although most employers probably won't want to hire an ex-offender, there are certain industries that are ex-offender friendly. We have included a list of some of them in Appendix B.

Phone interviews

In most cases, the hiring manager, a human resources person or someone else from the company you've applied to will call you for a phone interview. This will be your first interview, and if they don't like what they hear, it will be your last.

Usually the company will set the phone interview up ahead of time, so you can be prepared. And make sure that you *are* prepared. Learn everything you can about the company, the job you're applying for and the hiring manager. You can get this information on the company website, and you might be able to find information about the hiring manager by searching online using their name plus the company name or their name plus LinkedIn. Make notes, so you can refer to them during the interview. It's kind of like an open-book test.

If you can find a picture of the hiring manager online, call it up and talk to that photo, since you will sound more relaxed that way. Be sure to use a landline, if you can, because cell phones may be unreliable at times.

When you answer the phone make sure you answer with your name. For example, say, *"Hello, this is John Mason."*

Any phone conversation you have with anybody at the company, especially the hiring manager, should be considered a phone interview, since you're being evaluated.

Dealing with application forms

Employers often want job applicants to fill out application forms before they will consider them for an interview. These may be online or a paper application you fill out during the first time you visit the company. Whenever you fill out an application, be sure to refer to the master application that you have already completed and was explained in Step 2, so you don't make any mistakes. Do not leave a section blank if it doesn't apply to you. Instead write NA for "not applicable." Be sure to bring an erasable black pen, in case you are filling out the application manually and need to make any changes.

Try to avoid completing an application before you have an interview, if at all possible. First of all, these applications are used to weed people out. And secondly, nearly all of these forms ask if you've ever been arrested or convicted of a crime. You can lie, and say no, but if they find out—and they probably will since most companies do background checks these days—you won't get the job. Furthermore, an application form is a legal document, so if you lie about your record, you are committing fraud.

If you do get the job, and the employer finds out later, you will probably be fired. So the goal is to get an interview by networking, cold calling or whatever, before filling out an application form. You then have a chance to sell the employer on your skills and experience before having to inform them of your record. And even when you do talk about your record, you can explain how you learned from your mistakes and have turned your life around, as we will discuss in Step 5.

Another important reason not to lie is that if people find out that you've been incarcerated and your boss doesn't know, they could use that information to blackmail you. So be honest.

Remember to bring a post-it-note. Be sure to bring a post-it-note to your interview. At the time of your interview when you fill out the application, be sure to leave the question related to being arrested or convicted of a crime blank and fill out the post-it-note with the penal code and the year of your conviction. That way you can explain the situation in your turnaround talk, which will be explained in Step 5.

Another thing you want to be careful about is questions regarding salary or wage desired. You never want to put a dollar amount on the application. Instead write "negotiable" or "open." The reason for this is that you don't want to take the chance of putting in an amount that is less than the employer would be willing to pay. You also don't want to put in an amount that is too high and would price you out of the job.

Handling rejection

Rejection is part of the job search. It's going to happen. No matter how much experience someone has, they're not going to get every job they apply for. In fact they won't get most of the jobs they apply for.

You can expect to be rejected. But just like cold calling, it's all a numbers game. The more contacts you make, the more people you call, the more resumes or JIST cards you send out, and the more interviews you go on, the greater your chance of finding someone who will be happy to hire you.

One thing to keep in mind is that the two most important qualities you need as a job seeker are an ability to manage rejection and a determination to stay in the job search game. In essence, it's all about attitude. You may not have control over much of your job search, but you definitely have control over your attitude, and make sure it's positive.

How do you fish—in a barrel or in the ocean?

You can look at your job search as if you're fishing for a job. But are you fishing in a barrel or in the entire ocean? In other words, is your job search targeted, or is it all over the place?

If you're fishing in the ocean, you are:

- Spending most of your time looking at Internet job boards.
- Passing out your resume to anyone and everyone.
- Asking your friends and contacts if they know of any available jobs.
- Saying you'll take anything, you just need a job.
- Depending on people in your circle of contacts to find a job for you.

If you are fishing in a barrel, you are:

- Contacting hiring managers at the list of 100 companies you put together.
- Figuring out how you can help hiring managers solve their problems, rather than just looking for a job.
- Spending less than 20 percent of your time looking at Internet job sites.
- Calling hiring managers in companies you are interested in for informational interviews to learn more about their businesses.
- Walking into restaurants, retail shops or any small business and asking to see the manager, if that's the type of work you're after.

Want a job? Follow these examples:

Job seekers practicing out-of-the-box thinking are the ones who will succeed. Here are a few examples from workforce development expert Larry Robbin:

- A woman went into a retail shop and bought a cheap item. Pulling out her wallet to pay, she said that she wanted to speak to the manager, who appeared in an instant thinking there's a problem with the product. At that point the woman began to talk about her job search and what she could do for the manager if he hired her. He did.
- At the end of the interview for a warehouse job, a young man pulled out a notebook, saying he'd only been out of prison for two weeks but had been to apply in person at 240 places and showed him the list. Leafing through the pages, the hiring manager noticed his local Ace Hardware store and asked the ex-offender to describe it. He did, and the hiring manager was so impressed he hired him on the spot.
- In a job interview with a janitorial service one man asked why they didn't do forensic cleanup, the kind that happens after violent crimes. The employer replied that it's good work, but everyone they hired to do it in the past left because they couldn't stand dealing with the mess. A former medic in Vietnam who had seen terrible things, the job seeker said "if you hire me, I will build your forensics business." He was hired and did what he promised to do.
- People like to do business at places that hire those like themselves. One enterprising guy with disabilities went into a grocery store and told the manager that people with disabilities shopped at the competition. "Hire me and I'll get the disability market," he said. "I'll do publicity and distribute leaflets to potential customers." He was hired, and within six months 29 percent of the store's business came from people with disabilities.

STEP 4

Creating your network

"There is real magic in enthusiasm. It spells the difference between mediocrity and accomplishment."

– Norman Vincent Peale,
Author of *The Power of Positive Thinking*, which sold more than 15 million copies.

There's an old saying—"It's not what you know, but who you know"—that will help make you successful in life. And this is especially true when looking for a job. You need to know, or get to know, the type of people who can help you in your efforts. The average person in this country knows 200 or more people. You should too.

The best people are those who know you and already like you. They are more likely to understand where you're coming from and overlook your criminal record. They also might be more willing to recommend you to people they know.

No matter who you get to know, though, it's very important to expand your number of contacts as you look for a job. Many job experts say that most jobs are found in the "hidden job market." As we discussed in Step 3, you need to be able to find those hidden jobs by building a network of contacts.

No doubt you already have a network of some type. Start with family and relatives, neighbors, people you once knew, former classmates, ministers, shopkeepers you deal with, or anyone who is connected to other people in the community. Don't forget to consider your probation and/or parole officer as part of your network.

Circle of contacts

Workforce development expert Larry Robbin refers to a network as a circle of contacts. He suggests looking at it like a target. Put your name in the center—the bull's eye. Write the names of the people you are closest to—your family and best friends—in the first ring. Then put other friends, relatives outside your immediate family and maybe a minister in the next ring. Keep filling in the outer rings with more and more people you know but may not know very well. When you run out of people, your circle of contacts will be complete.

Job seekers find most jobs from their full circle of contacts. In fact, research shows that people tend to get jobs more from acquaintances than from friends. The chances are pretty good that you'll get your next job through someone you don't know that well or see very often. The reason for that is the people you know well will have many of the same contacts that you do, but those you don't know will have an entirely different set of contacts. You can learn more about Larry Robbin's Circle of Contacts in Appendix M.

Working persons inventory

You can also put together a "working persons inventory." Think of everyone you know and where they work. Zero in on those people who work in the type of jobs or companies you are interested in. Contact them, and tell them what type of work you're looking for or the type of company you'd like to work at, and ask if they have any advice for your job search. You can be more specific, and ask them what they would recommend you do to get a job in their field or in their company.

It's a good idea to include people who work for vendors who sell or deliver products to the type of company or industry in which you would like to work. For example, a UPS driver who delivers to warehouses and offices may hear about job openings, or see that a company is expanding by the increasing number of packages it is shipping out. A wholesale produce agent or delivery person is likely to know which restaurants might be doing very well and therefore expanding their staff.

Support group job leads

If you have gone or go to AA or NA, you will meet lots of people at those meetings who can be part of your network. You can ask to speak to the group, and many of them have a bulletin board at the back of their meeting room where you can post a notice that says you are looking for a job or your JIST card, which highlights your experience.

Job search networking group

Join a job search networking group. Many of them are connected to churches, and more and more churches are creating these groups to help their members and anyone else in the community who needs help with finding a job. These groups have regular meetings, usually weekly or biweekly, to help members keep the momentum. Ask at your local American Job Center about organizations in your area.

The meetings usually have a speaker who will talk about an angle of job searching. It may be something practical, such as how to use the Internet in your job search or the best way to write a resume. Or it may be a motivational topic, such as how to keep a positive attitude during the time you're looking for a job, so you don't get burned out.

The speaker will no doubt be interesting, but the real reason to attend these groups is to network and get to know people. The people in these groups are all looking for jobs, so they understand where you are coming from. They also have networks of their own and can refer you to people who might be able to help you.

Success teams. Many of these organizations also have what they call "success teams" that you may wish to join. These success teams are small groups of people, maybe five or 10 members, who get together each week to discuss their job searching experience. The meetings are a way for members to help each other out and make everyone accountable, so they stay on track.

Although these organizational success teams are usually for professionals, job seekers looking for any type of job can create their own job club or pair up with a job-hunting buddy. Find someone who is looking for a job. You might even be able to find a group of people. Maybe you can meet them through an American Job Center by asking one of the job counselors for the names of a few people who are searching for jobs similar to what you are looking for.

Social media

Facebook. It's not necessary, but you may want to create a Facebook account and make "friends" with as many people as possible, avoiding questionable characters. Use your account to let your friends know you're looking for a job. Be careful what you put up on the site, however, because it can harm you, as discussed in Step 3.

LinkedIn. You may also wish to establish an account on LinkedIn, which is used by many people to create job-related networks. LinkedIn members are mainly people with professional or white-collar jobs, so if you fit that description, you definitely should open an account and start inviting people you know to be part of your network. If you're a blue-collar or hourly worker, it's also wise to open a LinkedIn account. Since not many blue-collar or hourly workers have them, a LinkedIn account will set you apart from the competition and make you look more professional.

Professional organizations

Professional organizations can be very helpful for your job search. There are many types of these, but one of the best is the chamber of commerce.

Chambers of commerce. Learn about the chambers of commerce in your community. You can find your local chamber by searching online with the name of your town or city and "chamber of commerce." Most of them have monthly meetings and periodic "mixers," where members can network with each other. Some allow prospective members to attend. Chambers are usually made up of small businesses that are very active in their communities and can be a good source of job leads, as well as a chance to get to know people who may be able to help you in your search or even hire you.

The chambers also have membership directories. Sometimes these directories are printed, but these days most of them are on the chamber's website. Chamber directories are almost always organized by type of business. All contractors, for example, would be listed together. So you can go into the directory, click on a category and see all the members in that category with their contact information. Since chamber members are mostly small business owners, you can usually find the name of the company owner in the directory and call them directly.

Professional associations. Another place to look for contacts is through professional associations for specific types of jobs. There is an organization in the U.S. for almost anything, from bartenders and bathtub refinishers to caterers and carpenters. Many associations list their members on their websites, which can be searched by state and city, if they're a national association. You can use these directories as a way to collect names to contact. Job specific sites for professional and trade associations usually have job postings. The Riley Guide includes links to hundreds of association and professional websites that have job postings. Check it out at www.rileyguide.com/jobs.html. Click on a type of job and you'll see a list of associations for that job.

Depending on what kind of business you are in, a very creative way to meet people is to go to used-equipment auctions. These auctions are where small business owners and representatives of companies come to buy their equipment. This equipment could be anything from stoves for restaurants to moving equipment for construction companies. Search the Internet for auction company event listings in your area. Often these are also advertised in the newspaper or in the trade journals published for various industries.

Salespeople are another creative way to get contacts, since they deal with a lot of different people. Try to get to know some salespeople who sell products or services to your target market. They may be able to help introduce you to some of their customers.

Parole or probation officer

Make your parole or probation officer a part of your network. Sharing your turnaround packet with them is an excellent way to show that you have been rehabilitated and to make them a true advocate. Although they may not be able to give you job leads or even recommend you for a job, your parole or probation officer can be an excellent character reference and can share their experiences dealing with you. Be timely and pleasant in your dealings with them, no matter how they treat you.

The key is to let all the people in your network know that you are looking for a job. You never know who might know someone who has an opening for the type of job you are searching for.

Informational interviews

For some job seekers, a technique called an "informational interview" works very well. In an informational interview, instead of an employer interviewing you, you will interview them. This gives you a chance to talk to potential hiring managers—or even regular workers—about what it's like to work in their field.

Informational interviews are not used as often as they should be. It's a mystery why they're not, because this type of technique is a very good way to meet people and learn more about different companies and types of work. Many people are happy to participate in informational interviews, because they like to share information about what they do. A face-to-face meeting is the best kind of informational interview, but if people say they don't have time, see if you can ask them a few questions on the phone.

To set up an informational interview, you need to do the same sort of research you would do if you were trying to find potential employers. Choose a few companies to target and find out the names of potential hiring managers. Call them up, tell them you want to do an informational interview and schedule a time. These may take place at the person's office, or better yet, invite them out for coffee. The $4 or $5 it would cost is an excellent investment, and they often pick up the tab anyway.

You can also use friends to create contacts for informational interviews. If you know someone who does the kind of work you want to do, ask them who in their company might be a good person to talk to. Then when you call that person, you can say, *"So-and-so suggested I call, and I'd like to get together for an informational interview to learn a little more about the type of work you do."*

There is a certain type of etiquette that must be followed when you do an informational interview, however. These interviews are not about asking for jobs, but a chance to learn more about different types of work and different companies so you can decide what you might like to do. They also give you a chance to expand your network and meet potential employers and people who might be able to give you referrals to jobs in other companies.

Online forums

Online forums can be another tool to help you in your job search. Indeed.com, for example, is not just a great job aggregating website, but it also has great tools. You can use it to identify trends and salaries and to get advice on its online forums, where people go to share knowledge. These forums appear to be very effective. If you ask a question on the forum, people tend to be very helpful in supplying information about working in a particular company or field.

Job shadowing

Job shadowing goes a step beyond informational interviewing and can give you even better insight into a particular field or job. It is also a bit trickier to set up, however, and is not for everyone.

To job shadow means that you spend a day, or even longer, "shadowing" a particular employee as they do their work. This is particularly good for people who don't know exactly what they want to do.

For example, you know a lot about hand tools and are thinking about being a carpenter's assistant. Find a carpenter, and ask if you could "shadow" them for a day. You would go to their job site and watch what they do, maybe help out a bit in the process.

In order to job shadow you need the cooperation of the person you want to shadow, plus the permission of the company where that person works. Although this tactic takes time and effort to set up, it will provide a firsthand experience of what a certain type of job entails. And it will give you a new contact or two of people who are working in a field you might like to pursue.

Volunteering

Another way to expand your network of contacts is to volunteer. Volunteering may also offer a chance to learn some new skills if you choose the right organization or find helpful people to work with.

In addition, volunteer work is a way to get involved in something you really enjoy and to give back to the community where you live.

Make a list of what you like to do in your spare time and the things you are interested in. If you like to hike and camp, you might want to find an organization that is dedicated to preserving the environment or maybe one that takes urban kids on camping trips. Local food banks need help separating and packing the canned and packaged food items they receive. Soup kitchens need workers to serve meals to people who cannot afford to buy their own food. Habitat for Humanity is always looking for people with construction skills—or those willing to learn—to work on the homes its members are building.

There are endless opportunities to volunteer, and in a down economy when organizations have to lay off staff members because they don't have enough money to pay them, there are even more.

Volunteering for a few hours a week can be an excellent use of your time. It will lift your spirits and make you feel needed. It will give you new contacts and friends. And it may even give you experience in a type of work you might like to do and could possibly lead to future job opportunities. Most organizations use volunteers to help them do their work and are very appreciative of the people who help them out.

Temporary employment agencies

Another way to expand your network and polish up your skills is to work for a temporary employment agency. And you'll get paid as well.

Some short-term assignments from temporary agencies can turn into full-time job offers. Many employers like the temp-to-perm model, since they can check out peoples' abilities before hiring them.

Temporary agencies place everything from factory assemblers and warehouse workers to administrative assistants and accountants. You apply to work at a temporary agency, just as you would a regular job, by filling out an application form, either online or in person, and having an interview with a recruiter. Temporary agencies also give tests for certain types of jobs. These tests may be given to measure your typing speed, reading comprehension or basic math skills.

You can find temporary agencies by looking in the telephone Yellow Pages or searching www.whitepages.com online. Some agencies are national, with locations in major cities across the country. Others just have one or two offices in a certain area.

Employment agencies worth checking out

- Acrobat Outsourcing (www.acrobatoutsourcing.com)
- Barrett Business Systems (www.barrettbusiness.com)
- Command Center (www.commandonline.com)
- Labor Ready (www.laborready.com)
- Labor Systems (www.laborsystems.com)
- Labor Works (www.laborworks.com)
- Link Staffing (www.linkstaffing.com)
- Manpower (www.us.manpower.com)
- Nelson Staffing (www.nelsonstaffing.com)
- On the Move Staffing (www.onthemovestaffing.com)
- Staffmark (www.staffmark.com)
- Wollborg/Michelson (www.wmjobs.com)
- Workers.com (www.workers.com)

STEP 5

It's game time—How to ace the interview

"Good judgment comes from experience, experience comes from bad judgment."

– Mark Twain

All of your hard work over the past weeks has paid off. The hours you spent putting your list of potential employers together. The scores of phone calls you made. The number of times you visited company offices, stores, factories and/or restaurants. You're finally starting to receive calls for interviews. It's game time, and your goal is to make the best impression you can when you show up.

Dressing for success

There are many things you need to do to prepare for an interview—some of them way ahead of time. One important step in the preparation process is to think about your appearance, so you will look your best. Experts say that potential employers will make up their mind about you during the first few seconds after meeting you. They also say that appearance and body language make up most of that impression. So make sure you've got that covered.

Figure out the dress code of the company where you are interviewing, and dress appropriately. Don't dress too far up or down. For a carpenter or laborer-type job, you can wear casual clothes, such as khakis with a long-sleeve shirt. If it's a professional position where men would usually wear a coat and tie, do the same.

If you are a woman applying for an office job, wear a nice dress or a suit, depending on what you have or what you can get.

Don't overdress for the job interview, as it may appear that you are overselling or desperate. Many experts suggest dressing one notch above—or slightly better than—whatever one would wear on the job.

Free interview clothes. There are organizations that can help you get the clothing you need—and the confidence to wear it. These organizations were, in fact, created with just that purpose in mind.

Oakland's *Wardrobe for Opportunity* works on all aspects of helping men and women find and keep jobs. It supplies clothing and coaching to get ready for interviews but also goes way beyond that. Once a client has a job, the organization offers several programs to make sure they succeed. A six-week Pathways program helps participants develop communication and conflict-resolution skills. Wardrobe for Opportunity also provides one-on-one career coaching. A yearlong Success Series includes workshops, training and mentoring. Find out more at www.wardrobe.org.

In San Francisco, *St. Anthony's Foundation*, an organization that operates a dining hall and a variety of social programs also runs the St. Anthony Foundation's Free Clothing Program. The program provides all types of clothing to individuals but also gives away interview or employment apparel to both men and women. The organization's website has more information at www.stanthonysf.org/FreeClothingProgram.

Another organization, *Dress for Success*, with more than 100 affiliates around the world including one in San Francisco, supplies clothing and career advice to job seekers. Most Dress for Success affiliates, however, only work with women. You can find the nearest chapter at www.dressforsuccess.org.

Bay Area Women and Children's Center located in San Francisco's Tenderloin concentrates on helping women in that neighborhood. Among the many services it offers is the Free Clothing Closet, which has a special section of career clothing for women. After making an appointment, women can go and pick out complete outfits to wear to job interviews. To learn more visit www.bawcc.org/clothes_closet.

Before the interview

Now that you've made the effort to look your very best, you also need to prepare yourself mentally. Although interviewers make their first impression based on your appearance, what you have to say will convince them that you can do the job.

Plan. Spend a few hours on the day beforehand planning for the interview and what you might be asked. This is crucial because it will give you the confidence to be able to handle whatever questions the employer might come up with. A job counselor at an American Job Center should be able to help you with this. There are also many websites that have lists of typical interview questions and examples of how to answer them. One of the best of these can be found at jobsearch.about.com.

Practice. Read the questions, and answer them out loud. You may want to write down the answers to some of the more difficult ones and memorize them. The various job search websites list many, many questions, and the interviewer is unlikely to ask them all—or sometimes even that many of them. Practicing the answers, however, will help you focus your thoughts on your work experience and what you can offer the employer. It will also give you practice in dealing with job-related questions.

Role-play. An even better way to practice is to do it with someone, maybe a friend or family member. They can ask the questions, and you can answer them. This is called role-playing, and doing it will provide an opportunity for feedback. The person helping you can critique what you say, how you say it and the body language you use. Practicing in front of a mirror can be very helpful—in addition to or in place of role-playing. A mirror, however, won't give feedback on your performance.

No matter what you do and how much effort you put into it, you can never over-prepare for an interview. And this one may be the first of many, so it's important to get used to the process. Whatever time spent preparing for the first interview will pay off in subsequent interviews.

A lot of your success in an interview will depend on the "chemistry" between you and the hiring manager. Companies want to hire real, genuine people, so be yourself—your best self. Don't forget to be enthusiastic about the company and the position, but be sincere and don't go overboard.

Check out potential pay rates

You will also want to find out the pay scale for the type of position you're applying for if it wasn't advertised—and usually it's not. The best way to learn about pay for various jobs is to visit Salary.com or Payscale.com, two websites that are excellent sources of information on the subject.

At Salary.com you can do a search based on job title and the location where the job is located. The site's Salary Wizard will give you a salary range, so you'll have an idea of what the job should pay. Payscale.com asks for additional information, including your years of experience, what type of businesses you have worked in, your level of education and the name of the college you attended, if any. It then gives you a chart of the salary range for that position. JobStar offers a collection of over 300 salary surveys for a wide range of occupations and settings. It focuses on California and national surveys that can be found at www.jobstar.org/tools/salary/sal-surv.php.

You can also find out pay ranges by having conversations with people who work in the type of job you're applying for in your area. They can give you an idea of what people are paid in their field.

When the day arrives

The day of the interview requires a different type of preparation. You have to put yourself in a positive mood—to psyche yourself up to handle the interview. You can begin by thinking about a time when you felt completely confident and at the top of your game. Or you can imagine what that might feel like. Get in the mindset that you are an excellent candidate for the job, and you will get it. This confidence is crucial to guarantee that you will present yourself at your very best.

Power pose

Another thing you can do is called a power pose. It's the hands-on-the-hips wonder woman pose or what the athlete does when he raises both hands above his head to celebrate victory after crossing the finish line. Researchers have found that assuming a power pose for two minutes before going into an interview gives people the confidence they need to make a favorable impression. Go beyond the old saying "Fake it till you make it" to Fake it till you become it."

Be sure you know how to get to the place where the interview will be held. Use Google Maps to get directions or use a smart phone or use or borrow a GPS. Give yourself plenty of time. You should arrive about 15 minutes early, so you can relax a bit before the interview and begin to focus. Sit in your car for a while, or if you came by public transportation, walk around the block. Don't enter the office more than five minutes beforehand, however. Otherwise, you might be interrupting the hiring manager's work too early.

You're on—at last

One thing most job seekers don't consider is that an interview begins the minute they approach the office building or factory where it will take place. Be kind and smile at everyone you see. Be especially polite to the receptionist, since many employers check with them to see what they thought about the applicant.

Also be careful about what you are doing while waiting for the interview. Don't fidget or act nervous. If there's any literature about the company in the reception area, pick it up and read it. This will show that you are interested and paying attention to what's going on.

Smile. Go into the interview with a smile on your face. Nothing sets the right tone more than a smile and a firm handshake. Job search experts who have interviewed hiring managers say that hiring managers often decide whether to hire someone in the first five or ten minutes of the interview. So it's crucial to make a good first impression, and you only have one chance to do that.

Make sure you pay attention to how you walk into the interview. Don't shuffle your feet. Hold your head up high with your chin slightly raised, but don't look cocky or egotistical. It's not about power and entitlement. It's about looking confident, friendly and approachable, being just the kind of person they will want to hire. The power of a smile is an incredible motivating force.

Firm handshake. When you first meet the person or people who are going to interview you, offer your hand. Your handshake should be firm but not too strong. Be sure to make eye contact as much as possible. Some people recommend that you try to make eye contact two-thirds of the time. If there is more than one person interviewing you, switch your attention and eye contact back and forth between the various people during the interview. No one likes to feel ignored, and every person there will probably have a say in whether or not you get hired. One way to ensure you make proper eye contact is to notice the eye color of the people you're talking to.

More than words. It's extremely important to keep in mind that the words you use are just a small part of the way you communicate. It is said that the impression you make is based just 7 percent on the actual words you use, but 38 percent on the tone, pitch, volume and rate of your speech and 55 percent on your body posture, clothing, facial expressions and gestures.

Be excited and enthusiastic about the job without overdoing it. The most important thing is to come across as being sincere in your interest in the company, the hiring manager and the job. People hire people they like. So be likeable.

Always begin the interview by thanking the interviewer for the opportunity to be interviewed. Tell them you realize they probably have a lot of candidates and that you really appreciate being one of those chosen.

Provide short answers to hard questions and long answers to easy ones. Focus more time on the things you want to talk about. Although you can't control the interview, to a certain extent you can steer it in the direction you would like it to go. And that is on your strengths. Be prepared to elaborate on your strong points and what your skills, experience and talent can add to the job you're applying for.

Although some interviews may be very rigid, the best ones are like a conversation, with information shared back and forth. You want to make a good impression, but you also want to find out as much as possible about the job and the company to make sure it will be a good fit.

Come prepared with questions, such as "*Why did the person who had this job before leave? What do you feel are the most important skills and personality traits needed for this job? What do you feel is the most challenging aspect of this job? What is the best thing about working here?*"

The economic argument

Make an economic argument for them hiring you, not a social one. Convince them that hiring you will be an economic benefit. You will help them better their business.

Restaurant job. For example if you interview for a position as a busser in a restaurant, you can tell them that you will be very fast, so that tables can be cleared quickly and more customers seated. You will be very careful, so dishes and glasses won't be broken. And you will watch over the tables to help the waitstaff know which ones need more bread, water or whatever, instead of just clearing dishes.

Sales job. If you're interviewing for a sales position, bring along a list of 50 leads that you would call on during your first week on the job. This list can be developed from some of the same directories and resources you used for your job search. You would also want to talk about your closing skills and how you are pleasantly persistent. Through what you tell the hiring manager, you can paint a picture of how you are action-oriented and a problem solver—in other words, just the type of person they need to hire.

Even if you've never had a traditional sales job but have developed sales skills through your life experience, you still might want to consider working in sales. Sales people are some of the best paid of any occupation, and if you're successful at it, you have excellent job security. Employers look at effective salespeople as revenue producers and as an asset, not an expense. Also, in sales, a person's personality and persistence often matter more than their education level or other qualifications.

These are just two examples of how to paint a picture of your abilities. You can do this with any job—just use your imagination.

Keeping on track

Occasionally, especially in small- or medium-sized companies, you may get a hiring manager who doesn't really know how to conduct an interview. They may only hire an employee once a year or even less often. Maybe they've never hired anyone before. These employers may be very good at what they do, but interviewing people for jobs takes special skills, and they might not have them.

If you end up being interviewed by someone like this, be sure to keep the interview on track. Occasionally they may notice that you have an interest in common with them and want to talk about that in great detail. Or they may get sidetracked by something you said.

Take control. In this case, you have to take control of the interview, but in a very gentle way, by asking them questions about the job. You can say, for example, *"I'm really enjoying our conversation, since (whatever you're talking about) is of great interest to me. I'm afraid we'll run out of time, however, and want to know a bit more about this company and the job that I'm applying for. Can you tell me about ________?"*

They also might not ask any—or enough—questions about your background. In this case, you need to volunteer information. You can say something like *"I just wanted to let you know that my background is very suitable for this position, and here are a few reasons why."* Then tell them about your skills and experience and how these were applied in the jobs you held in the past.

Don't talk too much

Although you do want to bring the conversation around to your skills and experience and what you can contribute to the company, don't talk too much. Answer whatever questions they ask, giving just as much detail as necessary.

You definitely want to provide substantial information, but stick to the questions asked, and don't get sidetracked by talking about things not related to the job.

Some interviewers will pause at points during the interview just to see how the people they are interviewing handle silence. Being silent at certain points is not a problem. Sometimes people talk too much because they are nervous. Don't be one of them. Remember to talk about 20 percent of the time and listen about 80 percent of the time.

Another reason for not talking too much is because after a while you will begin to lose the interviewer's attention. So be careful to keep your answers on target. And watch the interviewer's face for any clues that they may not be listening carefully to what you're saying, or may be losing interest in you. That could be the worst thing that happens. If they're not interested in you, you won't get the job.

Illegal questions

Although employers can ask about your record, and you will learn how to handle that in the next section, they cannot ask you anything personal that is not job related. They cannot ask you about your religion, whether you are married or have children, your age, what year you graduated from high school or college or your sexual preference. Questions like these are illegal, because the information employers learn from them can lead to discrimination. They also can't ask if you've ever been arrested. They can only ask if you've been convicted.

Most employers are quite aware that they shouldn't ask these types of questions, but if they do, you can counter with something like, *"I'm happy to tell you my age, but first would you let me know how that is relevant to the job I am applying for." Or, if they ask about religion, you could say, "Would people who have a certain faith feel out of place here?"*

The turnaround talk

Eventually you will come to what could no doubt be the most challenging part of your interview—discussing your record. When you filled out your job application there was probably a question asking if you've ever been convicted of a crime. As explained in Step 3, you must answer this truthfully. A job application is a legal document and by lying on it you are committing a crime. Most employers do background checks these days and will find it out anyway. Whether they do a background check or not, however, if you lie and they discover it after you start the job, you will probably be fired.

So how should you deal with your record? It's not easy, but you need to turn your life experience into strength and a reason for a company to hire you. You've been through a lot and have overcome adversity, and as a result become a much stronger person. You have learned your lesson and decided to be a productive member of society.

You've already spent a lot of time thinking about how to handle this issue by putting together your turnaround packet. Now is the time to have what Larry Robbin, the nationally known expert in the area of workforce development, calls the turnaround talk. (See Appendix I for the actual formula.) It's better for you to bring this issue up before the hiring manager asks you a question that would force you to admit that you were incarcerated. The reason for this comes down to credibility. They might think that if they hadn't asked the question, you would have never brought it up. You want to be perceived as someone who would be as honest as possible.

Your story. Tell the hiring manager your story, very briefly stating the facts. You can begin by saying something like *"I want to tell you about what happened and what I've learned from the experience."* You should be completely straightforward, honest and sincere. Be sure to refer to yourself as a person in reentry rather than an ex-offender.

Don't talk too much about the crime you committed. Just briefly give the details and take responsibility for your actions. Tell them that you know what you did was wrong. Maybe it was bad judgment or happened because you were hanging out with the wrong crowd. Tell them that you've learned your lesson and know better now. Always be truthful and express remorse.

Carefully choose your words to allow the hiring manger to easily process your explanation of what you did. Just state the facts. You may want to tell them what you learned from your experience, and how you plan to handle things differently in the future. If the crime was violent or a sexual offense, you should express shame, remorse, and discuss what therapy and treatment program you have participated in.

Tell them about how you've turned your life around. Explain that you are not the same person you were when you committed the crime, however many months or years ago. Talk about the fact that you have served time and give details about any activities and classes you have participated in that show you are trying to improve your situation.

You should also try to convince the employer that what you have experienced in your life, including being incarcerated, has made you a stronger person with greater insight. And that gives you more to offer as an employee. Turn it into strength and an asset. In effect, the employer is ultimately getting a better employee because of your life experiences.

You may also want to say that you'd like to put that part of your life behind you—that it's in the past, and you're looking toward the future. Give examples of what you are doing now that will prevent what you did in the past from happening again. Maybe you've been to counseling, are regularly attending AA or NA meetings, have become a member of a faith-based organization or church, have new friends who are positive influences or have developed new skills that will help you find a good job.

Make sure to be extremely sincere and maintain eye contact with the employer.

When you tell your story is the time to pull out the turn-around packet (which is explained in Step 2 and in Appendix J) and say *"Here's proof. Here's what I've done to turn my life around and make amends."*

Also give the hiring manager an invitation to ask any questions they might have. And be sure to thank them for reviewing your turnaround packet.

Employer incentives

Another thing you might want to bring up is the fact that some employers can benefit financially by hiring ex-offenders.

Work Opportunity Tax Credit (WOTC). The WOTC is a Federal U.S. Dept. of Labor program, which promotes the hiring of people from specific target groups that experience barriers to employment. One of these groups is ex-felons, who must be hired no later than one year after conviction or release from prison.

The WOTC can provide an employer up to $2,400 in tax deductions for each qualifying hire and up to $9,000 for long-term-family-assistance recipient hires. Employers may claim a tax credit on an unlimited number of qualifying new hires! To find out more about the Work Opportunity Tax Credit visit the U.S. Dept. of Labor Employment & Training Administration website at www.doleta.gov/business/incentives/opptax/.

Applying for the WOTC can be extra work that some employers may not want to deal with. Large corporations have tax experts on staff who can do the work. Smaller or mid-sized companies might want to consider hiring a company like WOTC Solutions, which can do the process for a fee. Find out more at www.wotcsolutions.com.

The Next Step. You can also get help from The Next Step, a Shawnee Mission Kan.-based business, which manages the CoFFE (Cooperative of Felon Friendly Employers) database, a nationwide database of employers willing to hire ex-felons. The Next Step talks to employers about the financial advantages of hiring an ex-felon and also provides job seekers leads to ex-offender-friendly companies. It's just one more type of support that you can take advantage of. Find out more at www.thenextstep99.com.

The best thing to do is to visit your local American Job Center and talk to a counselor who can give you advice about these programs and how to approach an employer to talk about them. The counselor will help guide you through the process.

Federal Bonding Program. You can tell the employer about the Federal Bonding Program, operated by the United States Department of Labor. The program was created to insure such hard-to-employ people as ex-offenders, substance abusers and those dishonorably discharged from the military. It's the only program of its type and offers insurance to employers to cover acts such as theft, larceny, forgery or embezzlement that an employee might commit. The insurance ranges from $5,000 to $25,000 for a six-month period and is provided at no cost to the employer or employee. Find out more at www.bonds4jobs.com.

Filling out the application

These days many applications are filled out online before the interview, but you should do everything you can to try to get the interview first. The reason: applications are usually used to screen people out.

Many small- to medium-sized companies may still ask you to fill out a paper application when you arrive for an interview or after it's over. Be prepared to do so by bringing all the information you might need. Don't forget to bring a black pen or two. Not doing so will make you look very unprofessional.

Make sure you bring your master application, as discussed in Step 2, so the jobs and dates you list on the application form match those on your resume. You might want to go online and search for "sample job application form" to give you an example of what will be asked. You can print one and practice filling it out.

When you fill out the actual application form, make sure you read all the instructions carefully and think them through before putting anything down. Write very neatly. Answer all questions completely, with the exception of the one about your record. To answer that one, you should bring a post-it-note and write the penal code and the year of your conviction and attach it to the application.

Make sure that you take a proactive approach. If you haven't had many jobs, include volunteer work instead and treat it—on the application form, at least —just as you would a job, listing all the skills and duties you performed. Be positive and convinced that the skills you gained as a volunteer are transferable to the job you are applying for. They probably are.

If there are gaps in your employment, it's possible to list the jobs as having been performed during complete years, for example 2008–2009 instead of December 2008 to June 2009.

The "reason for leaving" column can be a bit tricky, but don't say you were fired unless you did something illegal. If you were laid off because of a downsizing or other reason, or even if it was because you didn't see eye-to-eye with the boss, give another explanation, such as "to take advantage of a new opportunity" or "to raise children." Don't lie, but find an alternative reason that works for you.

Be sure to sign and date the application, if it asks you to. Refer to your master application for the contact information for at least three references, because most application forms ask you to list them.

Correctly filling out the application is important, because part of the impression you will make is how you appear on paper.

In some cases you might be required to go in to fill out an application form in person before they'll even consider you for an interview. If you have to do this, come dressed appropriately (one notch above what someone in that position would wear to work), because they may decide to interview you on the spot.

See Step 3 for more information about filling out an application form.

Negotiating the pay

If you don't know what the pay will be, don't bring it up. Let them do that. If they ask you how much money you'd like to make, ask them what the pay range for the particular position is. You always want to let the employer make the first move on this one. If you mention an amount, it might be too low, and you might be paid less than you should be. Or it might be too high, and they won't want to hire you.

The pay scale is often advertised for hourly jobs, but in some cases, pay doesn't come up until they've decided to hire you. In every case, try to get the employer to tell you the pay range before you say anything.

Then you can say, for example if the hourly rate is $15 to $20 per hour, *"I've been looking in the $18 to $20 range, so that's just about right."* If they're talking in terms of an annual salary, and the range they mention is $40,000 to $45,000 per year, you can say *"I've been looking in the $40,000 to $50,000 range, so that's just about right."*

You've done your homework by checking Salary.com or Payscale.com (and by speaking with other people doing the same kind of work at similar businesses), and if the pay range they offer is lower than it should be and that's an issue for you, ask them if they're willing to be flexible by saying something like *"I really like this company and I'm sure I can do a good job, but this type of job in this area usually pays in the $18 to $20 per hour (or if it's a salary, in the $40,000 to $50,000 per year) range. Are you willing to be flexible when it comes to pay?"* They might say no, but it never hurts to ask.

Remember, however, with taxes the difference may not be as much as you think. Benefits, including health insurance, and vacation and sick pay, can outweigh additional pay. Sometimes getting your first job after incarceration is the ultimate stepping-stone to better things to come in the near future—promotions, other employment opportunities and peace of mind. As long as it is a living wage—or you are stringing together two or three part-time jobs to make a fulltime income—you should be satisfied. You also need to be realistic about income, particularly if it is your first job after being incarcerated.

Work for free

Although this is a radical tactic, it has worked for some people. If the employer seems hesitant to hire you, tell them you'll work for free. You can say something like this: *"I really want to work here, and I think I have the skills to do so. Tell you what. I'll work for free for a week or two, so you can see how good I am. Then, if you think I'm doing a good job, you can hire me. Would you be interested in that idea?"*

After the interview

Take notes during the interview about some of the important points that the hiring manager mentioned, or write them down as soon as you get out of the interview and into your car or on a bus.

Thank you note. When you get home, the first thing you should do is draft a thank-you note. A thank-you note will help you stand out, because most job hunters don't make the effort to create one. It is also a chance to sell yourself again or to get a second chance at a question you didn't answer very well.

You can send this thank-you note by email or U.S. postal service mail. Many experts feel that it's more effective to send a hand-written note through the U.S. mail, but in some cases the hiring manager might make a decision before the note arrives. To cover all bases, you might want to do both.

Send an email the day of the interview or the next morning. Write down a draft of what you're going to say in the thank-you note you will send by U.S. mail immediately after the interview. Let it sit overnight, read it with fresh eyes, write a final version and then send it.

Make sure that what you write in the email message and the hand-written note are different from each other. The email note could be longer and more detailed. You may want to begin the hand-written note by saying *"I'd like to thank you again for considering me for the (blank) position..."* Susan Ireland, author of *The Complete Idiot's Guide to the Perfect Resume,* offers some free thank-you letter templates on her website at www.susanireland.com that can be customized for specific employers.

Check in with your references

If you listed references in your job application, or if the employer asked for them, you need to call or email those people after the interview. By then, you should have a good idea of what the hiring manager is looking for, and you can tell your references to emphasize your strengths in those areas.

If you filed an online application or sent references with your resume before an interview, alert the people you are using as references as soon as possible. That way they will be prepared if someone calls. Sometimes companies check references before deciding to interview someone.

References can be very important, so choose them carefully. Make sure to thank them for agreeing to recommend you.

Follow up

Some experts say that less than 10 percent of all applicants actually return to places where they apply to check on their prospects of getting the job. In many cases, applying is only the beginning of the process. You must follow up. Keep going back at regular intervals (each week) to check and see what the hiring status is. Especially for entry- and mid-level jobs, this will show that you are interested, persistent and reliable. Don't be a pest though. Smile and be polite and look like you're ready to work at the company you're returning to. Doing this will set you apart from other applicants.

Improve your chances

Another good idea is have someone who respects you and knows you well—preferably a professional person—call the hiring manager on your behalf. That person should say something like *"I hear (your name) is applying for a position as (whatever you're applying for) at your company. He worked for me before (or he has volunteered for my organization or whatever), and I highly recommend that you hire him."*

This can be an incredibly effective tactic that surprisingly few people use.

If you don't get the job

Even if you don't get the job, it's important to follow up.

If the hiring manager calls you to let you know, ask them why they didn't hire you. If they send an email, call the hiring manager. Say *"I know you decided to hire someone else, but I just wanted to find out why I didn't get the job. I'd appreciate knowing the reason, because your feedback will help me in my job search."*

You may get feedback that could start a conversation and actually influence the employer to reconsider. That's rather unusual, but it has happened. Even if it doesn't, you may receive some valuable insight that can help you with future interviews. Being turned down happens to everyone at some point, so don't be discouraged. In fact, if you're not getting turndowns, you are likely not job hunting hard enough.

Each interview gets you more practice and closer to success. Looking for a job is a numbers game. The more potential employers you contact and the more interviews you have, the better your chances are of getting a job.

Highlight skills developed in prison

Being incarcerated may not have been the greatest experience, but it did help you develop some very useful skills. Larry Robbin, a nationally known expert in the area of workforce development, highly recommends that you bring them up during your interview.

Some that you will want to emphasize are the fact that you:

- Are able to function under pressure.
- Are experienced at getting along with all kinds of people. Tell the hiring manager you were never involved in a fight (if you weren't) and didn't get any time added to your sentence (if you didn't).
- Are skilled at following instructions. You are used to structure and routine.
- Are excellent at reading and interpreting body language, a very important survival skill in prison and a very powerful soft skill in sales and other jobs.
- Have knowledge gained from classes and training programs.
- Have skills gained from being a trustee—maybe you were given special responsibilities or were entrusted with mediation to solve fights or whatever.
- Have learned to be resourceful, to make something out of nothing and to be a problem solver.
- Have the ability to adjust to change.
- Are able to now see the bigger picture and appreciate the importance of having a job.

Four reasons why they don't want to hire you

Professor Harry Holzer of Georgetown University has conducted research and held focus groups on the most common reasons hiring managers do not want to hire people in reentry.

Here are the top four and how to deal with them:

1. **Cannot trust them.** Hiring managers fear that the person in reentry will steal or be dishonest. It's basically a character issue and important for you to tell them that you've never been arrested or convicted of theft—if you haven't.

2. **Feel unsafe.** They fear that the person will commit an act of violence. Tell them that you've never been arrested or convicted of a violent crime—if you haven't.

3. **Problem employee.** They're afraid that someone in reentry might commit a harmful action against a co-worker, customer or other person or against company property that could result in a negligent hiring lawsuit. Make sure you tell them that you are able to get along with all kinds of people and are a good team player. You could say that you were never in a fight and didn't get any time added to your sentence—if it's true.

4. **Fear that the person will go back to crime and be a retention risk.** You need to convince the hiring manager that you have turned your life around and want to move forward, not backward.

Six tips for landing the job:

1. **Make the hiring manager like you.** Make sure that by the time you leave the room you've found a way to convince them to like you. Establish a personal connection.

2. **Find a reason to care about the hiring manager.** Do your homework in advance. Check out their profile on LinkedIn and Facebook to see where they've worked and what their interests are. Try to find out more about them and their career in the interview. You want to ask questions about their professional, not personal, life. When you connect with them and start to like them, they'll start to like and care about you.

3. **Show them your passion.** Display passion for the job you're interviewing for. Passion and charisma go a long way. It shouldn't be difficult to do this, because you already did research beforehand and have a good idea of what is involved. You also need to tell the hiring manager what you can do to benefit the company and to help them solve their problems.

4. **Tell PAR (Problem Approach Resolution) stories related to your skills.** These include the **P**roblem you faced, the intelligent way you **A**pproached it, and its positive **R**esolution. Tell each story in 30 to 60 seconds. They can be from a job or a volunteer position and demonstrate how you are a problem solver. Hiring managers are not used to hearing PAR stories. Telling these stories can help move you to the top of the stack. They can be effective in resumes as well.

5. **Traffic-light rule for when it is your turn to talk.** The first 30 seconds, the light is green, and the hiring manager is paying attention. The second 30 seconds, the light is yellow, and the hiring manager may think you are rambling, or they are concerned that they will forget what they want to say next. The third 30 seconds, or 90 seconds into your answer, the light is red, and it is time to stop if you are still talking. You don't have to look at your watch, but just keep in mind not to talk too much.

6. **Unless you decide you don't want to work there, always, always ask for the job at the end of the interview.** In the language you feel comfortable using, you need to "close the sale." You can say something like,

"Based on what you shared with me, I believe this job would be an excellent fit, and I'd very much like to work here." If the hiring manager says something to the effect of *"We're still in the interview process until (date),"* say, *"May I follow-up on (date), if I have not heard from you?"* You want to come from a place of confidence but never sounding desperate.

Some of these tips come from Marty Nemko, career coach and author of *Cool Careers For Dummies.*

STEP 6

Fighting the enemy within

"I am convinced that life is 10 percent what happens to me and 90 percent how I react to it."

– Chuck Swindoll

In the job of job searching, you are the boss. You run the show and set the tone and the pace. Although there are many things you can't control, one thing you can is the wise use of your time. And effective time management is essential to a successful job search.

One of the most difficult things to do is to stay on track, stay focused and stay motivated. It's so easy to find more enjoyable ways to spend your time. You'll find countless reasons to put things off until tomorrow.

Or it's possible that you have just slipped into avoidance behavior. You may not be enjoying whatever you're doing, but you're doing it anyway just to avoid looking for a job. What can be helpful is to concentrate on the actual activity of your job search not the outcome. Don't think that it will be too hard or take too long. Just do it.

You may have a lot of other demands on your time. Dealing with a spouse. Raising children. Caring for an elderly parent. Life can be overwhelming at times, and the stress of looking for a job can make it even worse. It's easy to say you'll do things tomorrow. But don't get sucked into this mentality.

If you're working hard and not getting the results you would like, it may not be that what you are doing is wrong. Rather the way you are doing it may be the problem. Review your job search plan and see how it compares to the tips offered in this book.

You may need an attitude adjustment or to improve how you present yourself. Or maybe you've just been overlooking one or more of the most important steps. You might want to get together with your job search buddy or a family member or friend and role play the way you enter a room and conduct an interview, whether it's a face-to-face interview or one on the phone.

Most common job search mistakes

Larry Robbin, a nationally known expert in the area of workforce development, feels the most common job search mistakes are that the person:

- hasn't done enough consistent job hunting in a variety of ways.
- didn't practice job search skills, dress properly or work hard enough.
- had unrealistic job search goals in terms of jobs, wages, hours, etc.
- might not have been honest on the application or in the interview.
- cannot handle rejection.
- lacks the determination to stay in the game.

Nurturing positive thinking

If your job search is not going well, you need to re-examine the way you're thinking about what's happening. The more you talk about how bad things are, the more you are going to be mired in the problem. Neurons in your brain get bigger and stronger from negative thoughts and make it more difficult to move forward. The real answer is to take the next baby step toward what you want.

If you feel stuck, don't wait until you feel like changing. That rarely happens. Take a low-risk action. Behavior change usually comes before attitude change. Make the behavior changes first, and you will find your attitude changing.

We know a job search can be draining, but you have to work hard to be positive. You won't always get the first job you interview for. Or the second. Or even the third. People are hired for different reasons, and it's not always because they're the best. So don't take it personally.

Numbers game. As we said before, it's a numbers game. The more people you contact, the more interviews you go on, the better your chances are of getting a job. Just work on your job search all day, every day. It's like planting seeds. Eventually those seeds will sprout and bear fruit. If you don't get a job, go back and review what happened in the interview. Call the hiring manager and ask why they didn't hire you. They may tell you, which can be valuable advice on how to do things better the next time around.

Don't get discouraged. Failure is part of the game. No one really succeeds without failing. You can only control your effort, not the outcome. Some of the most famous people in America and elsewhere failed before they succeeded. They succeeded because they refused to let failure defeat them. Instead they looked at it as a learning experience and modified what they did so they would be closer to succeeding when they tried again.

Here are some examples that may inspire you to keep going:

Soichiro Honda couldn't get a job as an engineer at Toyota Motor Corp., but instead of giving up he began building scooters in his home and went on to found Honda Motor Co.

Babe Ruth struck out 1330 times before he made it to the Baseball Hall of Fame.

Elvis Presley, who became one of the top recording stars of all time, was fired from the Grand Ole Opry after his first performance there and was told, "You ain't going nowhere son. You ought to go back to driving a truck."

Oprah Winfrey's road to television superstar had a few bumps along the way, including being fired from a job as a TV reporter and told, "You're not fit for TV."

Theodor Seuss Giesel, more commonly known as Dr. Seuss, wrote some of the greatest childhood classics, including *"The Cat in the Hat"* and *"Green Eggs and Ham,"* but his first book, *"To Think that I Saw it on Mulberry Street,"* was rejected by 27 publishers.

Abraham Lincoln lost eight elections, failed at two businesses, and had a nervous breakdown before becoming our 16th President.

Michael Jordan was cut from his high school basketball team during his sophomore year.

The enemy within

Self-doubt and procrastination are the worst enemies of job seekers, and it's very important to learn how to deal with them. We already talked about procrastination in Step 3. Now it's time to address self-doubt.

To deal with self-doubt, if that's a problem, you have to have a serious talk with yourself. Tell yourself that you have talents and skills that would benefit employers. That you're hard working and reliable. That there's definitely a job out there for you—you just have to find it.

Just do it. It's essential to create a mindset focused on action. As the Nike slogan, says "Just do It," and that should become your mantra. Don't tell yourself it's too hard. Don't try to talk yourself out of accomplishing your goal for the day. Just do it.

To actually do something, no matter how small, is essential to getting the ball rolling. One of the best ways to stay on track is to get up in the morning as soon as you wake up. Lying in bed will only make things worse. Eat a good, well-balanced breakfast and take a walk, or do some exercise to wake up and get your mind in gear. Some people drink coffee, but exercise is a much healthier option for launching your day. Celebrate the baby steps. Even if what you do seems small or unimportant, it's a step in the right direction.

Getting support

Although it's already been mentioned, creating a job search team, finding a job search buddy or joining a group of other people who are looking for work will help keep you on track.

Get together with your job search buddy or group once a week and share your plans. Let everyone know what you have been doing and what you plan to do for the week ahead. Tell them how many—and the types of—companies you are contacting. Ask advice on your resume. Practice your elevator pitch. Get the others to ask you the types of questions you might encounter in an interview. Be polite and nonjudgmental, but be honest. Give constructive criticism to each other. Otherwise, you're wasting your time. If you don't have a job search buddy, you can do the same thing with a spouse, a partner or a friend.

Finding motivation

Practical ideas are useless without motivation, but once you get motivated you also have to carry out your ideas.

Ask yourself what's the most fun aspect of looking for a job. Is it the opportunity to meet new people? The chance to explore the area and learn about various businesses? The pure challenge of the hunt? The success you'll feel when you land the job?

Make it a game. There are some ways you can make the process more enjoyable. Turn your cold calling list into a chart and keep track of your activity. See how many hiring managers you can call in one day. See how many appropriate businesses you can find within a 10-mile radius of where you live. Make it a game—a contest where you are competing against yourself to do things better and more efficiently. Try to make it fun.

Reward yourself. Give yourself a reward each time you make your daily cold calls. The reward could be anything that brings you pleasure—a treat to eat, a walk in the park, a call to a friend, a few minutes on Facebook (but make sure you give yourself a limit of maybe 30 minutes, so you don't spend too much time checking out what all of your friends are doing).

Think about the benefits you will get when you land the job. You might be able to move to a better place, go out more often or buy something you haven't had the money for up to that point. Also consider peace of mind. You will have achieved your goal and won't have to look anymore. You are likely to have some of your own benefits to add, as well.

Handling stress

Stress seems to be an integral part of our lives today. In this speeded-up, do-it-yourself world, there are so many demands on our time, and so many things to do. It's difficult, if not impossible, to accomplish everything, even though you try as hard as you can. Instead of being able to accomplish everything you set out to do, you become stressed out and irritable.

One way to handle the kind of stress that may be caused by procrastination is to begin by doing something you know you can accomplish. It may be a five-minute—or even a one-minute—task. However long it takes, this low-risk action will give you a sense of accomplishment and get you going.

You can only control what you do, not what happens with what you do. You can control the number of resumes and JIST cards you send out and the quality of those resumes and JIST cards. You can control the number of cold calls you make and who you make them to. You can't control the response you'll receive from the other side, however. They may get back to you, or they may not. They may be interested in meeting you after a phone conversation, or they may not.

Do what you can to make things happen, and then let it go. It's all a numbers game. The more letters, resumes and JIST cards you send out, the more chance you have of a response. The more hiring managers you call or visit, the more likely you will find one who is willing to talk to you.

Try mindful meditation

One serious cause of stress is an obsession with the past. You may be thinking about all the bad things that have happened to you and play them over and over again like a movie in your head. You may be dwelling too much on the time you served or the crime you committed.

You may also be worrying about the future, about the difficulties of finding a job, what will happen to you or your family, the fear of returning to your former life.

These thoughts, however, are counter-productive. The past is past. It's over. Forever. You can't change it. You can, however, control the future to a certain extent by the actions you take today.

Even if you understand this, negative thoughts can still get in the way and keep you from moving forward. One way to deal with these negative thoughts and be able to move forward is through a practice called mindful meditation.

Meditation. Meditation helps your breathing and heart rate slow down. It clears your mind for a few minutes and helps you relax. It can also help increase self-confidence and positive emotions.

You might think of meditation as something that Buddhist monks do in monasteries—sitting in rows, each in a lotus position. Meditation is basic to Buddhism, but it is also becoming a popular practice among regular everyday people. It can help you to center yourself and take you away from those negative thoughts. It can also help you slow your heartbeat. Doctors are beginning to recommend meditation to their patients to help them reduce stress.

Some scientists have found that meditation stimulates the left prefrontal cortex of the brain. That is the part of the brain associated with positive feelings and happiness. In fact, researchers at the University of Wisconsin who studied a group of Tibetan monks found intense activity in that part of the monks' brains. Their research shows that you can train your brain to help you think more positively and be happier.

Meditation is not difficult to learn, and you'll get better as you practice it. Here's how to begin.

Breathing. Gradually bring your attention to the present moment. You can close your eyes or focus on a point in front of you. Begin to focus on your breath, breathing normally and naturally. Concentrate your awareness at the tip of your nose or your abdomen. If you're focusing at the tip of the nose, feel the touch of the air as you breathe in and out.

If you're focusing on your abdomen, feel your belly contract when you inhale and expand when you exhale. As you breathe in, be aware that you are breathing in, and as you breathe out, be aware that you are breathing out. Concentrate on the present moment.

Just feel your breath. There is nothing to figure out. There is nowhere to go. There is just being in the here-and-now, noticing your breath. Just living your life, one inhalation and one exhalation at a time. Breathing in, breathing out, watching each breath appear and disappear. Just breathing.

Now, release your awareness of the breath and bring attention to the body, feeling the sensations within. Acknowledge your body's many sensations moment-to-moment.

If you come across areas in your body where there is tightness, allow it to soften, if possible. If the sensation remains and persists, however, then just let it be there, remaining and persisting. Observe the waves or resonating rings of sensations, just letting them flow wherever they need to go.

Try to let your mind be like a meteorologist, just watching the internal weather patterns without judgment. Just be with the way things are. Sensations rise, sensations fall. Watch them appear and disappear.

Focus on your mind. Now release awareness of sensations and bring attention to your mind: to thoughts and emotions. Observe your mind without making any judgment. Just acknowledge the multitude of varying mental formations moment-to-moment. Think of this exercise as if you were lying on a field and watching the clouds float by. Watch the mind in the same way. Thoughts rise. Thoughts fall. Watch them appear and disappear.

Release the awareness of the mind and bring your attention to your hearing. Observe the sounds. Be aware of sound at its most basic, fundamental level. Acknowledge the multitude of varying sounds internally or externally, moment-to-moment. Sounds rise. Sounds fall. Listen to them as they appear and disappear.

Now come back to your breath and feeling your body as you breathe in and out. Feel your entire body rising upwards as you inhale and falling downwards as you exhale. Feel the body in its entirety, connected and whole.

You're done. Over time this can help you feel more relaxed and able to be more focused. It's not that difficult, but the more you do it, the more effective it will be. You will need five to 20 minutes of distraction-free time to meditate. In the beginning, you will also probably need a quiet place, but as you do it more you will be able to meditate anywhere.

You can begin each morning with a meditation session to get the day going. You can use free time throughout the day to meditate. Maybe you'll arrive early somewhere and have a few extra minutes to meditate in your car. You can also meditate before going to bed. Many people say meditation helps clear their minds, so they can sleep better.

No matter where you do it or how often, meditation can help you improve your thinking—and can help you become more focused and at ease, so you can effectively conduct your job search.

Be thankful

Instead of feeling down and depressed when you're looking for a job, be thankful. What? Be thankful, you ask? Be thankful for what? You're out of a job, having trouble paying the bills, didn't hear back from the last 20 companies you contacted. Yes, it's tough looking for a job, but it's also a great opportunity. So look at the situation in a different light, and it could change the way you approach your job search. This new outlook might even lead to success. It's all in the attitude.

Being thankful is a great thinking-outside-the-box idea that comes from an executive recruiter named Harry Urschel, who writes a blog called "The Wise Job Search." You can read his posts at www.thewisejobsearch.com.

An opportunity. Instead of being down and depressed, look at your job search as an opportunity. It's an opportunity to get to know yourself better. How often in your life will you take the time to sit down and really figure out what makes you tick? To be able to find out what you really like to do? To discover what your life's purpose is to be through your work? This won't happen very often, so be thankful.

This is also an opportunity to learn the skills it takes to find a job. And job hunting, especially in a tight market, takes real skills. This will no doubt not be the last time in your life that you are going to have to look for a job. Some experts say that people change careers—not jobs—seven times in their lives. So get prepared to be ready to do this again in the future. And be thankful for what you are learning now.

A job search is an opportunity to get out and meet new people, to develop networking skills and to explore new career opportunities. It is also a chance to reinvent yourself, which is probably the most important thing of all for ex-offenders.

Be thankful every day for the opportunities your job search gives you, and see if your new attitude doesn't change your entire approach to looking for work.

STEP 7

"The best way to make your dreams come true is to wake up."

–Muhammad Ali

Pursuing other options

You may have tried to find a job for a while and haven't been successful. Or maybe you would rather try a different approach from the beginning. In either case, there are other ways of getting a job besides those that have already been described in this book.

We will discuss three of them here—job training by nonprofit organizations, apprenticeships and starting your own business.

Job training and placement programs

If you have been incarcerated—or haven't worked—for a long time, a job training or apprenticeship program may be the way to successfully reenter the workforce. Job training programs are usually offered by nonprofit organizations or occasionally by churches.

Goodwill. One of those job-training programs, the Goodwill Academy, is for those who don't have much work experience. It provides paid job training at the organization's 25 stores and three processing plants in the East Bay region, which includes Alameda, Contra Costa and Solano counties. You can find out more at www.eastbaygoodwill.org or by calling 510-698-7200. For other locations, contact www.goodwill.org or 800-GOODWILL.

Delancey Street. Delancey Street helps those who have hit rock bottom—ex-offenders, drug addicts, prostitutes and alcoholics—get back on their feet. The organization operates a residential program, with facilities in San Francisco, Los Angeles, New Mexico, North Carolina and New York. Five hundred people live in Delancey Street's complex on the San Francisco waterfront.

Delancey Street is open to all ex-offenders with three exceptions—those who have committed arson, those forced to register as sex-offenders and those on psychotropic drugs.

During the first weeks of the program, residents work doing building maintenance and serving meals. They then earn their way out of maintenance and into a vocational training program. These programs cover a wide range of skills and businesses, from accounting and automotive repair to construction work and catering. Graduates have gone on to start their own businesses and work at top-notch companies.

Although Delancey Street residents receive no pay, food, housing and clothing is provided. The money made from the businesses it operates is put back into the organization. The program is not for everyone, however. It demands a certain amount of isolation from the outside world. Residents are not allowed to write to their immediate families until after the first month. They can only make a phone call after 90 days.

The process for being admitted into Delancey Street's program is straightforward and does not take long. Those who go for an interview and are likely candidates are accepted on the spot. You can find out more about Delancey Street at www.delanceystreetfoundation.org or by calling 415-512-5104.

Dr. J. Alfred Smith, Sr. Training Academy (JASTA). This academy, run by East Oakland's Allen Temple Baptist Church, runs six- to eight-week classes teaching students about the construction and culinary trades. In addition, it offers mentoring and help with preparation for the GED test and has a career center where people can take computer classes. Staff members also give advice on getting into the green jobs program at Laney College. You can find out more about the academy at www.allen-temple.org or call 510-544-8910.

Volunteers of America Bay Area. This local branch of the national spiritual-based nonprofit Volunteers of America operates, among other things, programs for low-risk ex-offenders. It provides 120-day to one-year live-in programs at two residential communities, Elsie Dunn and West House, with training on such things as job search techniques, anger management and life skills. Its Project Choice, operated in conjunction with Oakland's Measure Y Initiative, offers pre-release services and individual and group counseling to those 18 to 30 years of age returning to Oakland. For more information, visit www.voa-sac.org or call 916-442-3691.

California New Start. An initiative of the California Department of Corrections and Rehabilitation, California New Start was created in 2009 to help those still in prison and those already released to find employment. The New Start Transition Program operates in four California prisons—Folsom State Prison, R.J. Donovan Correction Facility in San Diego, California State Prison Solano in Vacaville and Valley State Prison for Women in Chowchilla—where it conducts 70-hour four- to five-week programs in job search techniques.

For those in reentry, the program works with 24 Workforce Investment Boards, including Alameda County, San Francisco and Oakland, to fund training on how to find a job. To learn more, contact the Office of the Community Partnership at 916-327-4901.

Center for Employment Opportunities (CEO). This organization, with offices in Oakland and San Diego as well as New York and Tulsa, helps people coming out of prison enter the workforce by giving them life skills education, short-term paid transitional employment, full-time job placement and post-placement services. You can learn more about the organization at www.ceoworks.org or 510-251-2240.

America Works. An employment service with a difference, this company partners with hard-to-place individuals in construction, retail, telemarketing, transportation and food jobs. It also provides job readiness training that concentrates on soft skills, computer skills and issues like anger management. Find out more about what it does at www. americaworks.com or 510-891-9100.

If you're not located in the Bay Area, check with your local American Job Center for similar organizations in your area.

Apprenticeship programs

One way to learn a new trade and get paid while you're doing it is to join an apprenticeship program. These programs are for jobs that offer decent wages.

Apprenticeships provide both classroom and on-the-job training and pay participants a portion of what they will earn in the future while they are training for a new career.

In order to participate you must be 18 years old and able to perform the type of work the trade requires. You also may have to prove that you are a high-school graduate or produce a GED certificate. Another requirement is being able to read, write and speak English, along with proof that you are a United States citizen.

There are about 35 different trades that have apprentice programs registered with the California Division of Apprenticeship Standards (DAS). That means that these programs meet certain standards set by the state government. The trades range from carpenter and meat cutter to plumber and automotive technician. Some are more affected by economic ups and downs than others. Be careful to choose a trade that is currently in demand—or will be so in the near future.

The length of the apprenticeship program depends on the trade but can last several years. When you are finished, you will receive a certificate of completion issued by the California Division of Apprenticeship Standards (DAS). In addition to the certificate you will be officially recognized as a journeyman or journey worker. Both of these have meaning and will help you gain respect in the eyes of potential employers and local, state and federal governments.

Since apprenticeships are sponsored by unions, they will also prepare you to be a successful union member and give you access to union jobs.

Rigorous training. These apprenticeships are a great way to prepare for a job, but they can also be very rigorous. The plumber's apprenticeship program, for example, requires a five-year commitment, during which apprentices must work 9,000 hours of on-the-job training and attend 1,080 hours of training classes.

The carpenter apprenticeship program requires a minimum of four years, with 4,800 work hours and the completion of 612 hours of instructional classes taken at a Carpenters Training Center.

For more information and to explore the apprenticeship options available in California, visit www.calapprenticeship.org.

You can find apprenticeship programs in other parts of the U.S. by checking out the U.S. Department of Labor Office of Apprenticeship Sponsors at oa.doleta.gov. The office's database includes apprenticeships for every state. The site has a pull-down menu, where you can choose a county to see what companies or organizations—or for some jobs even military units—have registered for that county. Just because they're registered with the Department of Labor, however, doesn't mean they have apprenticeships available when you contact them, but it's definitely a place to start. And they may be able to steer you to a nearby county or another program if they don't have anything currently available.

Government training programs

Both the federal government and many state governments have money to invest in job training. Most of these funds are for specific types of jobs, but it may be something you will want to look into.

Workforce Investment Act training. The Workforce Investment Act provides job training to qualified adults for a variety of jobs for which there is a demand in the marketplace. Although the act is a federal act, the services are administered through state employment offices. In the case of California, it is through the Employment Development Department. To learn about these training programs, you should visit your local American Job Center.

If you are eligible to enroll in a training program and decide to do so, you will learn the skills necessary for the job you are being trained for, but that is not enough. Many people go through these programs and still can't find a job. It's up to you to be proactive in your job search, be enthusiastic in your interviews and work hard to find the job once you've been trained how to do it.

Do-it-yourself training

In the brave new world of at-your-fingertips access to information thanks to the Internet, there are unlimited free or inexpensive opportunities to learn a wide variety of basic or advanced level computer and information technology skills. Many of these skills, including a basic knowledge of Microsoft Word and Excel, are necessary for some of the jobs you might be applying for.

Learning Word and Excel. Although classes in Microsoft Word and Excel are taught at community colleges and local adult education centers—almost every city has one of these—a more efficient way to learn these two programs is on your own. If you, or someone you know, has these programs on a computer that's the best option, but you can also go to a public library, sign up for a computer with the longest session possible (in many places that's two hours), and get to work.

Microsoft has a training website where you can learn Microsoft Word, Excel and 10 other programs, including PowerPoint and Outlook, all of which you may need to know for an office job. The other programs, like Access, Project and Publisher, are for jobs that require advanced skills. All of the learning tutorials on the website, however, are set up in a similar way and include step-by-step instructions on how to use various aspects of the programs. The videos can be viewed online or downloaded as PowerPoint slideshows. To access them, visit office.microsoft.com/en-us/training and click on the program you would like to learn.

Self-employment

Starting your own business may take a lot of work, but it's definitely an option if you are hard working, are full of good ideas and have an entrepreneurial spirit. Many people, in fact, prefer to work for themselves than someone else. It is estimated that 10 percent of all working Americans are self-employed, so you won't be alone. For a lot of ex-offenders, creating a job for themselves might be an easier way to go.

There's an old saying about businesses: "Find a need and fill it." And there are many needs in today's society that need to be filled. As people get busier and busier, they're hiring out more and more of the things they used to do—everything from yard work to meal preparation—to others who are willing to do the work for them.

Explore options. If you have a special skill or interest—whether painting houses, making sandwiches, dog walking or trimming trees—think about what kind of business you could build around that skill. Brainstorm a few ideas, and go talk to people in other towns about the type of business you might be interested in. Don't talk to people in the area where you want to start the business, because they may look at you as potential competition.

Another route might be to decide what type of business you'd like to start, and get a job with someone who is doing that kind of work. Then when you have the experience, start the same type of business in another area.

Initial investment. In choosing a business, you'll have to figure what the initial investment would be for equipment, office space if needed, supplies and advertising. For some jobs, you might need a truck to haul tools and equipment. For others, you might have to buy specialized equipment. After deciding what type of business to start, make a list of everything you'll need to start that business and find out how much it would cost to buy it. Then add up the total and try to figure out where you will get the money to pay for it all.

Look into micro-lenders. If you don't have enough capital to launch a business or if you start one and find out you'll need more money, consider contacting a micro-lending organization. You may have heard of this type of group, which traditionally has given small loans to people like Peruvian farmers, African craftswomen or street vendors in India. Micro-lenders are now busy funding businesses in the U.S. as well and give loans of $500 to $100,000. Opportunity Fund in San Jose is one of these. It provides loans at low fixed-interest rates to Californians who want to start or expand businesses but can't afford to do so on their own. Find out more at www.opportunityfund.org.

Finding customers. Don't forget that when you have your own business you're not just doing the work, but you also have to find customers, which is sometimes the hardest part of the job. Many customers will come by word-of-mouth from people who were pleased with your work. You may also want to create a website for your business.

Another way to find customers, especially if you have a service business such as house painting, window cleaning, gutter cleaning or screen repair, is to make up a simple flyer describing what you can do and distribute it on the front porches of homes, preferably in affluent neighborhoods. This flyer doesn't have to be fancy. Just type up the services you can provide on a computer document —you don't need any fancy graphics—and print the flyers from your computer or print one and take it to your local copy shop to do photocopies.

Business possibilities. Here are some businesses to consider that don't require extensive startup costs, although most of these do require a vehicle:

- Chimney sweeping
- Handyman service
- Janitorial service
- Firewood service
- Graffiti cleanup
- Hauling service
- House painting
- Mobile auto body and dent repairing
- Dog walking
- Shoe shining
- Tree trimming
- Yard work
- Errand services
- Personal assistant
- Housekeeping
- Elder care–conversation and companionship, transportation
- Window washing and rain gutter cleaning

For more ideas go to http://www.entrepreneur.com/businessideas/index.html or search for "business ideas" and see what you come up with yourself.

A couple of businesses you can start with little money, for example, are house cleaning and yard work. Once you start working for someone, you can ask them if they need help with anything else and maybe get more work. You can also ask if they know of anyone else who might need your services. Doing this type of work is especially good if you don't have much experience or have gaps in your resume.

Become a recycler. One business that you may want to consider is to be a recycler. You would need a truck to haul the items, but it should be a rather straightforward business to set up. You can create a flyer of what you pick up for recycling with your contact information (phone number and email address), make copies of it and deliver them to homes in affluent neighborhoods. The flyer would say what day you'll be through the neighborhood picking things up and what you are willing to take—everything from water heaters and washing machines to cell phones and car batteries.

You can also pick up e-waste such as laptops and monitors, but if you want to make money at this, you need to apply to the California Department of Resources Recycling and Recovery to participate in its CEW (Covered Electronic Waste Program). To access an application visit the department's website at www.calrecycle.ca.gov/electronics/Act2003/Recovery/Application/#Application.

Start a food cart business. Another business possibility is to run a food cart business. You could do this selling coffee and desserts from a cart in a large office building or hospital or on the street. You'd have to check out the local permits for this, however, and, if it's inside, negotiate with the building owner or manager.

Become an urban farmer. As more and more people are eager to eat locally grown and organic fruits and vegetables, a new business model is arising. Some entrepreneurial types are growing produce to sell at farmers markets or to restaurants. You can create a garden to do this in your yard if you have one, at the home of a friend or even in a vacant lot. If you live in a rural area, it might be even easier to find a place to grow things.

There are several programs that teach people how to be farmers. *The Garden Project*, located on the grounds of the San Francisco Jail, offers apprenticeships to ex-offenders. During the program they will learn how to grow organic vegetables and get help with computer skills and literacy and possibly attend community college classes. You can get the details at www.gardenproject.org.

In West Oakland, a nonprofit, *City Slicker Farms*, offers three-month internships and yearlong apprenticeships that teach people the skills needed for urban farming. The organization oversees seven community market farms that have spaces open to the public, more than 100 backyard gardens and a greenhouse. Find out more about what it does at www.cityslickerfarms.org.

Public storage company auctions. Another interesting business that you can do on the side while you're putting together another business is to go to public storage company auctions. These companies auction off items in storage units when people don't pay the rent on those units. You never know what you will find at these auctions, and you can bid on items and then take them to sell at flea markets or on Craigslist or eBay.

Join a chamber of commerce. Another way to get work is to join a group like the local chamber of commerce in the area where you are doing business. Each chamber of commerce has a website listing all its members and the type of businesses they do, and many people like to hire companies that are members of their local chamber.

Jumpstart your business

If you do decide to start your own business, there are many people and organizations that can help you put it together. They provide great resources that are often low-cost or no-cost.

Small Business Administration. The Small Business Administration, which maintains offices in every major U.S. city, offers a series of workshops, most of which are free. These workshops deal with everything from accounting issues and how to use the Internet for marketing to getting organized and increasing sales. For more information go to www.sba.gov.

Renaissance Entrepreneurship Center. The Renaissance Entrepreneurship Center provides classes, low-cost, one-on-one consulting services and a business incubator with low-priced office and cubicle space. For more information check it out online at www.rencenter.org.

Women's Initiative. Women's Initiative offers an intensive 20-session training program known as *"Simple Steps to Business Success"* in both English and Spanish at its training centers in the Bay Area and New York. The course helps low-income entrepreneurs create a business plan and learn to carry it out. The organization also has a revolving loan fund, giving loans of $1,000 to $25,000 to some of its participants. Although it's called Women's Initiative, 2 percent of its clients are men. If you're interested, check out www.womensinitiative.org.

Service Corps of Retired Executives. Another place to turn for help is SCORE, the Service Corps of Retired Executives. This organization is a resource partner of the Small Business Administration. It matches successful former business owners with entrepreneurs who are just starting out. SCORE offers free and confidential business advice through online and face-to-face mentoring. Learn more at www.score.org.

APPENDIX A

Top five ways to hunt for a job

These techniques offer the best results, according to career expert Richard Bolles, author of *What Color Is Your Parachute?* Utilize at least two of these techniques when hunting for your job.

1. **Ask for job leads.** Ask family members, friends and people in the community if they might know somebody who knows somebody who works in a company that you're interested in or might work in a place that has the type of job you'd like to do. Your contacts are key, and your next job is likely to come from someone you know or a person someone you know knows. When you do this, be sure to use the circle of contacts that we describe in Appendix M.

2. **Knock on doors.** Visit factories or offices that you think you might want to work at, whether they have jobs available or not. Avoid the human resource department. Talk to the manager of the department you're interested in working in. This person is typically referred to as the hiring manager. Tell them about your skills, and ask for their advice. If you make a good enough impression, you'll have an inside track when it comes time for them to hire someone. They even might create a job for you, if they like you enough. But the odds are small that this will happen, so you have to visit as many companies as possible. It's a numbers game.

3. **Make a List.** Use the Yellow Pages, either online or in the phone book, to help determine the types of jobs that might be of interest to you. Make a list of 100 employers and call at least 10 per day. Speak with the hiring managers of the departments you're interested in about your qualities for the type of

Please note: Although the contact info in this book primarily targets the San Francisco Bay Area, you can find organizations similar to those listed throughout the United States. Your local American Job Center (www.servicelocator.org) and public library (www.publiclibraries.com) can help you locate them. Also, your local public community college career center (www.utexas.edu/world/comcol/state) can be helpful and should be open to the public, whether you're enrolled as a student or not.

position you can do and do well. (And don't forget to pursue companies that have 20 or fewer employees, since they offer two-thirds of all new jobs.)

You can also use the American Job Center's Employer Locator, which can be found at www.careerinfonet.org/employerlocator, to build your list of 100 employers. Search by industry, occupation, location, keyword and firm size (number of employees).

Once a job is advertised there is much more competition. Career expert Marty Nemko states that "cold calling and creating your own leads, except for the highest level positions, is the most potent strategy."

4. **Apply to temp agencies.** Temporary employment agencies can be a good option too. Some short-term assignments can turn into full-time job offers. Many employers like the temp-to-perm model, since they can see what kind of workers people are before hiring them. Temp agencies place everything from factory assemblers and warehouse workers to administrative assistants and catering and food service workers.

5. **Find a job hunt buddy or join a job club.** Team up with someone else who is looking for a job or create your own job-hunting club with other job hunters. Hang out with positive people. Share ideas, provide emotional support to one another, talk by phone and even meet one or more times each week.

APPENDIX B

Ex-offender-friendly businesses

This is an alphabetical listing of types of businesses that have hired people in reentry, along with a few job types that might be suitable for ex-offenders. This list does not include every type of employer who has done this, so don't limit yourself to just what is listed below. And remember, there is no guarantee of a job for someone in reentry—or anyone else for that matter.

- Advertising promotion and flyer distribution companies
- Animal shelters
- Apprenticeship programs
- Asbestos removal companies
- Assembly lines
- Bakeries
- Cab companies
- Cable TV, contract door-to-door sales canvassers
- Car wash operations
- Carpet installation companies
- Charities
- Churches
- Construction companies
- Courier services
- Crime scene or forensic cleaners
- Day laborers
- Delivery services
- Department stores
- DirecTV, contract door-to-door sales canvassers
- Drug and alcohol counselors
- eBay sellers
- Environmental clean up companies
- Faith-based organizations
- Factories
- Fast food restaurants
- Food prep/counter work at delicatessens

- Food processing plants
- Gang diversion programs
- Garbage collectors
- Gas stations
- Golf courses
- Government agencies
- Greenhouse workers
- Grocery stores
- Hardware stores
- Heating and air conditioning companies
- Homeless shelters
- Housekeeping services
- Janitorial services
- Junkyards
- Landscaping services
- Lumberyards
- Machine welding and metal fabrication shops
- Maintenance companies
- Manufacturers
- Motels
- Moving companies
- Newspaper delivery services
- Nonprofit organizations
- Nurseries (trees, plants, etc.)
- Oil and gas drilling companies
- Oil changing businesses
- Petition gatherers
- Pizza and food delivery
- Recycling centers
- Refineries
- Restaurants
- Roofing companies
- Sales (outside and inside)
- Security guards
- Sheet metal companies
- Solar energy companies
- Staffing agencies

- Temporary agencies
- Thrift shops
- Tire shops
- Towing services
- Transmission shops
- Transportation services
- Trucking companies
- Warehouses

APPENDIX C

Resume examples

There are two basic styles of resumes. One is the chronological resume. This type lists the jobs a person has held in the order they have held them. It includes the job title, the company and location, the dates a person worked there and the duties of the job. The most recent job is listed at the top.

A functional resume is a list of a person's skills. Under each skill heading are bullet points with descriptions of how these skills were used in whatever jobs a person has held. A combination functional/chronological does both, and it is the best choice for many of those in reentry, since it can be used to cover up gaps in employment or is effective if you are looking for a job that is different than what you have done in the past.

You can check out an example of a chronological and a combination functional/ chronological resume on the next two pages.

Chronological resume example

Jack Pierson

245 Crestwood Drive, Tioga Hills, CA 94556
(123) 555-1234 jpierson339@whatever.com

Carpenter's assistant with a variety of skills gained from experience in home construction and remodeling projects

CARPENTRY SKILLS

- Window and door framing
- Ability to read blueprints
- Good communication skills
- Cabinet and appliance installation
- Experience with hand and power tools
- Valid drivers license

EXPERIENCE

Anderson Builders Inc., Oakland, Calif., April 2008–December 2011

- Assisted carpenter with residential remodeling projects, including kitchens and bathrooms.
- Erected scaffolding, shoring and braces.
- Delivered equipment, tools and materials to construction sites.
- Helped install cabinets.
- Assisted with window and door framing.

Gold Star Construction, Berkeley Calif., January 2006–March 2008

- Assisted carpenter by holding timbers and paneling.
- Fastened lumber with glue, nails and screws.
- Helped carpenter by holding equipment.
- Cleaned work areas and machinery.
- Performed a variety of duties as requested by carpenters.

EDUCATION

Laney College, Oakland, Calif., Classes in carpentry department

Chronological/functional combination resume example

Jack Pierson

245 Crestwood Drive, Tioga Hills, CA 94556
(123) 555-1234 jpierson339@whatever.com

Carpenter's assistant with a variety of skills gained from experience in home construction and remodeling projects

CORE SKILLS

- Window and door framing
- Ability to read blueprints
- Good communication skills
- Cabinet and appliance installation
- Experience with hand and power tools
- Valid drivers license

EXPERIENCE

Carpentry
- Assisted carpenter with residential remodeling projects, including kitchens and bathrooms.
- Erected scaffolding, shoring and braces.
- Helped install cabinets.
- Prepared and helped with window and door framing.
- Assisted carpenter by holding timbers and paneling.
- Fastened lumber with glue, nails and screws.
- Helped carpenter by holding equipment.

General Support
- Delivered equipment, tools and materials to construction sites.
- Cleaned work areas and machinery.
- Performed a variety of duties as requested by carpenter.

WORK HISTORY

Anderson Builders Inc., Oakland, Calif. April 2008–December 2011
Gold Star Construction, Berkeley, Calif. January 2006–March 2008

EDUCATION

Laney College, Oakland, Calif., Classes in carpentry department
Oakland Tech High School

APPENDIX D

JIST card

The JIST card, which was discussed in Step 2, is like a mini-resume. In many cases it can even be more effective than a resume, since it allows you to emphasize your strong points and doesn't show any gaps in employment.

JIST stands for Job Information Seeking and Training, and the concept and the card were invented by the late Michael Farr, who was a career expert and author.

A JIST card basically includes your name, contact information and a summary of your experience in a paragraph. You can use this paragraph to highlight the work you've done and the skills you've developed. Since there is no list of the jobs you have held, a JIST card doesn't show any periods that you weren't working or even the names of the companies you worked for.

The beauty of a JIST card is that not only is it unique, but it also has nothing that can be perceived as negative, and you can send them out with a cover letter instead of a resume.

Like a resume, a JIST card is just a key to open the door to a face-of-face meeting or interview. According to some studies, resumes only get a cursory glance of a few seconds each, which is hardly enough time to really see what a job applicant has to offer. In the same amount time, a hiring manager can see a snapshot of what you have accomplished from a JIST card.

In order to create a JIST card, sit down for a brainstorming session and write down your best examples of job experience and skills. Then write up a paragraph describing them, as in the example below. Since your JIST card is just a quick summary, be sure to only focus on the things that you think the hiring managers will find most impressive.

JIST cards are usually 3″ x 5″ but can be any size. You can get perforated card stock divided into 3″ x 5″-sized cards from an office supply store and print them on your computer then tear them apart.

Another way to make JIST cards is to set up a template on a computer and get them printed and cut at a copy shop. If you don't know how to create a template, get help from someone who does. You'll probably want to make at least 100 to begin with, but you can always do more later. While some people recommend printing them on pastel-colored cards to help them stand out, like in the case of resumes, white is more professional. Just the fact that it is a JIST card will make it distinctive.

Once you print the JIST cards, you can:

- Send them out with a cover letter instead of a resume.
- Leave one with the receptionist or better yet the hiring manager, if you walk into a company without an interview.
- Give them to local businesses that might have contacts with suppliers.
- Hand them out to family and friends.
- Email employers with your card as a PDF or Word attachment.
- Include two or three cards with each hand delivered application.
- Take them to job fairs.
- Send them out with a cover letter instead of a resume.
- Bring extra cards for in-person interviews to leave with the interviewer.
- Include one with each employer thank you note you send.

Here's what one should look like using the same information as the resumes in the previous pages:

Jack Pierson
Position: Carpenter's assistant

Phone: (123) 555-1234
Email: jpierson339@whatever.com

Four years of experience in a variety of home construction and remodeling projects, including window and door framing, cabinet work and appliance installation in projects that included kitchens and bathrooms. Experience with a wide range of hand and power tools, skilled in reading blueprints, able to communicate effectively and an excellent problem solver.

Hardworking, reliable, honest and cheerful.

APPENDIX E

Difficult interview questions

Hiring managers are likely to ask difficult questions, so you must prepare ahead of time and practice answering some of them. That way, if you are asked one or more of these questions, you won't be caught off guard and can answer them effectively.

These questions are general questions. You will learn how to handle your record in Appendix H, which is about dealing with criminal records.

Tell me about yourself. This is where you give your elevator pitch, and remember to keep it brief. About 15–30 seconds is sufficient.

What is your greatest strength? They may ask for your two biggest or three biggest strengths, so be prepared with several examples.

What is your greatest weakness? Again they may ask for more than one.

Why would you like to work here? That is for you to decide.

What do you know about this company? Make sure you do your homework and learn as much as you can about the company where you will be interviewing.

Why should I hire you? Think in terms of how your efforts can help the company improve its products or service and ultimately make more money.

How do you handle stress? Think of an example of a past situation to illustrate how you handle stress on the job. If you've developed a meditation practice as described in Appendix P, then mention it here.

What are you passionate about? Make sure this answer relates at least somewhat to the job. For example, if you're applying for a retail or restaurant job, you could say *"I'm passionate about people. I love to meet them, talk to them and make them happy."*

How do you describe good customer service? This question is particularly likely to be asked by retail or restaurant managers.

If we asked people who know you why you should be hired, what would they say?

What would your last boss say about your work performance?

How do you evaluate success?

What type of environment do you prefer to work in?

Describe a difficult situation you had in a job and how you overcame it. This is where you tell your PAR (problem, approach, resolution) story as explained in Step 5.

There seems to be gaps in your work history. What were you doing during that time? These gaps could be related to your time in jail or prison, so you'd give the turnaround talk, but there may be other gaps as well. As for the turnaround talk, it's better for you to bring that up before they ask, if possible.

What is your hourly pay (or salary) expectation? If they ask this question, reply with something like, *"What is the pay range for this position?"* You don't want to state an amount, because you might be under-pricing or overpricing yourself. Try to get them to answer first.

Do you have any questions? Be sure that you come to the interview with a handful of questions about the company or the job itself. You could ask the hiring manager things like why they like to work there, what qualities make a good employee at their company, etc. You can also ask why the last person left or is leaving, if you don't know already. Questions are important. If you don't ask anything, the hiring manager will either think that you aren't interested or that you haven't done your homework.

APPENDIX F

Top interview tips

G.E. Miller, a man in Michigan who writes the 20somethingfinance.com blog and works at a Fortune 500 company where part of his job is to interview potential employees, has some excellent information for job searchers.

We were so inspired by his Top Interview Tips we'd like to share them with you and have thrown in a few ideas of our own as well.

Personality is more important than a resume. Although a resume may be the key to get you in the door, once you have the interview, your personality is what really matters. Be genuine and sincere. Highlight experiences that show who you really are. That's what they want—to get to know the real you. Maybe you can fake it and be someone else, but that won't last once you get the job.

How you answer is more important than the details you include. You need to make a serious effort to answer the questions, and if you don't understand what the interviewer means, ask. Take notes that you can refer to later and, most important of all, be confident, or at least act like you are.

Be enthusiastic but not desperate. Don't be insincere by lavishing too much praise on the company, but make it clear you'd really like to work there. Otherwise you shouldn't be interviewing for the job.

Ask smart questions. Prepare beforehand and ask some smart and unique questions. If you do your homework and learn about the hiring manager, you can ask them things related to their own background. And never, ever ask about pay. Always let them bring that up first. Bringing it up yourself may make it look like that's the most important thing, and it shouldn't be.

Show that you're adaptable. If you worked for one company and had several roles, that shows you took the initiative to learn and grow. A history of several different jobs using different skills shows the same. If you feel strongly that you have skills that you haven't used before but are relevant to the job at hand, elaborate on them.

Highlight a few of your nonwork activities. This is a chance for you to talk about things you've done for organizations—or maybe even just for fun. Miller uses the example of an applicant who participates in open mic night at a local comedy club in order to improve his public speaking skills and stretch his creativity. Maybe there's a similar situation for you to talk about.

The interviewer is not out to get you. Interviewers are not out to highlight your weaknesses or put you down. In fact, they really want to be able to hire you, since then their work of considering potential employees will be complete, and they can get back to their real jobs (unless they're human resources managers, for whom interviewing is part of their job).

Make eye contact and smile. By making eye contact and smiling at points throughout the interview you're creating a connection and establishing rapport with the interviewer. Miller says he wants to feel comfortable with applicants and wants them to feel comfortable with him.

Stand up and offer a handshake at both the beginning and the end of the interview. Doing this will establish rapport with the hiring manager and show confidence on your part. It's also a sign of respect. It may seem a little old-fashioned to some readers, but a firm handshake shows professionalism and confidence, so do it.

APPENDIX G

Employer incentives to hire ex-offenders

There are financial incentives available, in particular the Work Opportunity Tax Credit, that might encourage employers to hire you. Make sure you understand what they are and can present them to the hiring managers in the job interviews you go to.

Work Opportunity Tax Credit (WOTC)

The WOTC is a Federal U.S. Dept. of Labor program, which promotes the hiring of people from specific target groups that experience barriers to employment. One of these groups is ex-felons, who must be hired no later than one year after conviction or release from prison.

The WOTC can provide an employer up to $2,400 in tax deductions for each qualifying hire and up to $9,000 for long term family assistance recipient hires. Employers may claim a tax credit on an unlimited number of qualifying new hires! To find out more about the Work Opportunity Tax Credit visit the U.S. Dept. of Labor Employment & Training Administration website at www.doleta.gov/business/incentives/opptax/

Applying for the WOTC can be extra work that some employers may not want to deal with. Large corporations have tax experts on staff who can do the work. Smaller or mid-sized companies might want to consider hiring a company like WOTC Solutions, which can do the process for a fee. Find out more at www.wotcsolutions.com

The Federal Bonding Program

Under the auspices of the U.S. Dept. of Labor, this program provides fidelity bonding for the first six months of employment for hard-to-place job applicants, including ex-offenders, without any cost to the employer or job applicant. This bonding is basically insurance to cover employers for any loss of money or property because of dishonest actions by its employees.

If you are seeking bonding services and/or a job you should call 877-872-5627 or check the website www.bonds4jobs.com for:

1. The location of the nearest workforce office/American Job Center, and

2. The phone number of your state's State Bonding Coordinator. Some states don't have a State Bonding Coordinator, and if you live in one of them, you will be referred to the nearest American Job Center for assistance.

APPENDIX H

Dealing with your criminal record

Step 1: Know what is in your record! You will need to know the following for each conviction, so that you can find out if any mistakes were made and so that you will know how to deal with the information in your job search:

- the case number
- the court (Alameda County Superior, Oakland, etc.)
- the code section violation (e.g. penal code section 459 or H&S code section 11377)
- the sentence (e.g. three years probation, $100 fine, etc.)
- the sentencing date
- the length of probation and when probation ended (if any was given)

Step 2: Order your Summary Criminal History (aka, your "Rap Sheet" of all California records of arrests, convictions)! If you have multiple convictions (or questions), order your Rap Sheet by requesting a "Record Review Packet" by going to http://ag.ca.gov/fingerprints/security.php. To order an application for your DOJ Summary Criminal History:

- Call 916-227-3849, 916-322-2209 or 916-227-3835. You will need to leave a message requesting an application packet.
- Or write to: California Dept of Justice, P.O. Box 903417, Sacramento, CA 94203-4170. Attn: Records Review Unit.
- Request a Record Review Packet, an application for fee waiver and a fingerprint card, if you want to reduce the cost for ordering (otherwise you will be sent a Livescan form, which costs $25–$75 to process).
- Once you receive the packet, fill out the form and fee waiver, get fingerprinted (at police stations and other locations – costs approximately $10), and send in these items. Your request will be processed and sent back to you within six weeks.

Step 3: Get legal assistance! Get assistance in the county in which you were convicted, if you are applying for expungements and/or reductions (or the county where you live, if applying for a Certificate of Rehabilitation).

1. If you had a public defender for your case, the public defender's office will assist you in applying for relief (expungement, sealing, reductions, and Certificates of Rehabilitation).

   a) Convictions in Alameda County: The Alameda County Public Defender 510-268-7400.
   b) Convictions in San Francisco: Operation Clean Slate, San Francisco Public Defender 415-553-9337.
   c) Convictions in Contra Costa County: Contra Costa Public Defender 925-335-8000.

2. If you had a private attorney, often this attorney will help you apply for relief and may not charge you, so call them.

3. If you are not eligible for the public defender, or have questions, call Suitcase Clinic Legal Services at the East Bay Community Law Center (Alameda County only) at 510-548-4040 ext. 366.

Step 4: File your motion with the court! Once you have all the necessary information and know what relief you are eligible for, file your motion(s) and supporting documents with the criminal court clerk of the superior court. A hearing will be held approximately 30 days from the day you file your motion(s) and a judge will make a decision to either grant or deny your motion.

More information can be obtained from the California Department of Justice website Criminal Records Request page at http://oag.ca.gov/fingerprints/security.

More information and programs can be found at the following:
Rubicon Legal Services is a Contra Costa-based provider of legal services to low-income residents with a variety of situations, including the formerly incarcerated. Find out more information about the Richmond-based center on its website at www.rubiconprograms.org or by calling them at 510-232-6611.

Clean Slate Clinics
Find out all your legal options for dealing with your criminal record! Free legal services are available to help you prepare to have your convictions dismissed or reduced for those eligible. Also, learn how to respond to questions about past convictions. Learn what employers can legally ask regarding past convictions.

Alameda County:
Wiley W Manuel
Superior Courthouse
Self-Help Center, 2nd Floor
661 Washington St.
Oakland, CA 94607
Tuesdays & Thursdays
9 a.m. to 12 p.m.

Eden Area American Job Center
24100 Amador St., 3rd Floor
Hayward, CA 94544
Wednesdays
11 a.m. to 12 p.m.

East Bay Community Law Center
2921 Adeline St.
Berkeley, CA 94703
www.ebclc.org
510-548-4040
This clinic, run by UC Berkeley Boalt School of Law students gives free legal advice for those who wouldn't be able to pay for it otherwise.

Alameda County Clean Slate: 510-548-4040 ext 357.

Contra Costa County:
Office of the Public Defender
3811 Bissell Ave.
Richmond, CA 94804
510-412-4900

Office of the Public Defender
800 Ferry St.
Martinez, CA 94553
925-335-8000

Get Your Rap Sheet:

California Rap (Covers All California Counties)
Write to: California Department of Justice
P.O. Box 903417
Sacramento, CA 94203-4170
Attn: Records Review Unit
916-227-3849 or 916-322-2209 Leave Message

Alameda County Sheriff's Department
15001 Foothill Boulevard
San Leandro, CA 94578-1092
510-667-7721

Office of the Sheriff Contra Costa County
Records Unit
500 Court St.
Martinez, CA 94553
925-335-1570

Get help cleaning up your record.

The Papillon Foundation is a tremendous resource for those who qualify and would like to try to expunge their arrest or conviction record(s). Its website offers a wide range of information, with links to forms, articles, how-to guides, organizations and free legal resources for all 50 states, the District of Columbia and the American Territories.

This organization will also give free personal help to certain ex-offenders—those who are indigent, a veteran or a victim of human trafficking—if they need it. For everyone else, it asks for a small donation.

The Papillon Foundation
P.O. Box 338
Creston, CA 93432-0338
805-712-3378
www.papillonfoundation.org

APPENDIX I

The turnaround talk formula

Larry Robbin, a nationally-known expert in the area of workforce development, has created the idea of ex-offenders presenting a turnaround talk as part of their job interview process.

We talked about this in Step 5, but because this is so crucially important, we'd like to go over it again and offer more details.

The ultimate goal is to turn your experience of being incarcerated into strength and a reason for the hiring manager to offer you a job. In spite of the fact that we refer to people as ex-offenders in this book, you should refer to yourself as being in "reentry" and not as an ex-offender.

The turnaround talk is so important because it offers you a chance to give examples of what you have learned and how you have changed your life. You can talk about volunteer work you've done, new friends you've made who are helping you out in your job search, and new attitudes you've developed that have made you a better person.

Practice your turnaround talk with family, friends, counselors and, if possible, with people you don't know very well, because those can be some of the best practice sessions since the person who will interview you doesn't know you either.

When you are preparing your turnaround talk, be sure to consider the following:

1. Be polite and begin by thanking the hiring manager. After the interview gets going, you've established rapport and they ask you about your employment background, tell them *"There's something else I'd like to bring to your attention."* Or *"Before we move on, I just wanted to let you know about my life situation and give you a little bit of information about myself."* Then lead into your turnaround talk.

2. Make sure you don't blame anyone else or deny what you did. Explain your situation. Depending on what happened, you might want to just say that you were part of a bad crowd; that your parents stopped supporting you and you were forced to live on your own; or that you did something without thinking, learned your lesson and wouldn't do it again.

3. Give a brief explanation of the facts. Make it clear and simple, with no "trigger words." If the crime was not work related be sure to include this fact in your explanation. Instead of talking about burglary, say you took some things you shouldn't have taken. If you were a drug addict, say you had a substance abuse problem and, if true, you went through a recovery program and are fully cured. If you were an alcoholic, say you had a drinking problem and, if true, you went through a recovery program and are fully cured. If you attend AA or NA meetings or other 12-step programs, be sure to mention that. If you killed someone, say you took a life. If you were arrested for assault, say you hurt someone. If you dropped out of high school, say you left school early. You get the picture. Think about what you did and how to rephrase it in more gentle terms.

4. Express extreme remorse, and be sorry for whatever crime you committed. Show them that you understand what you did in terms of how it affected the victim, their family, your family and yourself. When you do this, you need to make eye contact and use appropriate body language.

5. Establish a trust account. Explain to the potential employer how they can know it won't happen again. Tell them what you have learned from the experience and what you have done to turn your life around. Include any activities you've participated in that prove you are trustworthy.

6. You need to build a trust account to counter stereotypes concerning why people in reentry don't get hired, the most serious of which is that employers *can't trust them not to steal.* From the employer's perspective, you need to have a "trust account." With no work history or if you have gaps in employment, you have NO trust account. You must make deposits into this account in as many of the following ways as possible:

- Explain that you were a “trustee in the jail” (if you were).
- Discuss positive things you did while incarcerated, whether it was completing a GED or college courses or participating in a work program.
- Show that you were granted early release—for work, volunteering or whatever (if that is true).
- Share testimonials from your parole or probation officer, etc.
- Give examples of volunteer work and community service you have performed.
- Display evidence of restitution.
- Provide proof of contributions to child support.
- Show participation in victim reconciliation.
- Prove that you are going to school (if you are).
- Document participation in rehabilitation programs.
- Demonstrate your desire to have a fresh start by sharing your goals.
- Explain that if they hire you, they can get a $2,400 tax credit and that you can be bonded for up to $5,000 at no charge to the employer. Check out www.jailstojobs.org/incentives.html to get the latest information.

7. Ask them if they have any questions, and tell them you’ll be happy to answer them.

APPENDIX J

The turnaround packet

To go along with your turnaround talk, you should put together what Larry Robbin calls a "turnaround packet."

What to do with it. You will show this packet to the hiring managers who interview you, because it includes information that is intended to turn the potential employer's perception of you around and make them realize you would be a good employee.

Why you should create one. You want to convince the hiring manager that the person you were when you committed the crime is not the person you are today. And your turnaround packet demonstrates that and clearly shows you have been rehabilitated.

It's quite a lot of work, but your potential employer is sure to be impressed that you took the time and effort to put all the information together. It is also a very organized way to state what you've done to improve your life and gives you a lot of positive things to talk about in your interview. In addition, the process of putting together the turnaround packet and sharing the information in the interview can be a very positive experience and give you more confidence for your interview.

How to make one. Put as many of the turnaround packet items listed below as possible into a binder or a file folder. Ideally each example should be in its own plastic sheet protector to keep everything neat and orderly. A typical turnaround packet is six to eight pages, starting with the first page where you put basic information about yourself and a note to thank them for the interview.

The Turnaround Packet could include some—or all—of these things:

- Four letters of reference - two of these should be from people who acknowledge the fact that you have a conviction. It is better to ask for references from someone, such as a former employer or landlord, who is used to evaluating people, rather than someone, such as a clergy member or social worker, who will write a reference for anyone.

- A clean printout from the DMV, if you have a good driving record. Visit your local DMV office, and for a small fee they will to print one out for you.
- Letters from groups you've done volunteer work for.
- School enrollment forms.
- Certificates of completion of training programs (both pre- and post-incarceration).
- Honorable or general discharge papers from the military, if you served. If it was a dishonorable discharge, don't include it.
- Photos of your accomplishments as a volunteer.
- Copies of award certificates or other forms of recognition.
- If you have to go for a drug test, take along containers of the prescription drugs you are taking to show them.
- A copy of a clean drug/alcohol report, especially if you were arrested for drug use or have been in an alcohol or a drug rehab program.
- Documentation of restitution, if you had to pay restitution to a victim or victims.
- Photos of any hobbies or interests you might have, such as car or motorcycle restoration, dressmaking, artwork, furniture refinishing, gardening or whatever.
- Be sure to only include items that show you have been rehabilitated and do not draw attention to areas that still need work.

APPENDIX K

Job search websites

There are quite a few job search websites, and each of them is slightly different from the others, so you have to get to know them to learn which ones will work for you. Some people check the sites every day, but except for Craigslist, which tends to have a lot of listings, this is a waste of time. A more efficient method is to spend a few hours one day of the week to conduct an online search and look at all the sites at the same time.

General job search sites

Craigslist.org. This community bulletin board is organized by city and includes everything from personal ads to items for sale. Checking out this site is a must for job hunters, since many employers only advertise on Craigslist. There are scores of jobs listed every day in categories ranging from general labor and government to tech support and transport. While some websites only specialize in professional positions, this one has it all.

Careerbuilder.com. Although Careerbuilder.com tends toward professionals, it does have listings for carpenters, mechanics and maintenance jobs, among others.

Monster.com. At one time, Monster.com was the most popular job search website, but the cost of placing an ad there has caused many employers to look elsewhere. The site includes all levels of jobs and is still popular with some employers, so include it in the sites you search.

Careeronestop.org. This website, run by the U.S. Department of Labor allows you to explore careers, learn about salaries and get advice on how to put together resumes. It also links to state job banks, where you can look for a job.

Job aggregators

Indeed.com, Simplyhired.com, Linkup.com. These three sites are what are called aggregators, and they draw listings from other sites, including company websites. Indeed.com, Simplyhired.com and Linkup.com have listings that others don't and should be a regular part of everyone's job search. They all work the same way and may have some of the same listings, but each one pulls job postings from different places, so it's worth it to check them all out. Each is keyword and ZIP code searchable, and you can sign up for job alerts just as you can with other Internet job boards.

Government job websites

USAjobs.gov. This website lists most, but not all, federal jobs. It includes a database of jobs that can be searched by keywords and by city, state or ZIP code.

DCjobsource.com. This is also a government job website but a bit different than USAjobs.gov. It contains a list of links to federal agencies, most of which have jobs listed on their sites. Many of the jobs listed by these agencies do not appear on USAjobs.gov. If there's a certain type of job you're interested in, find out which agencies might hire people who do that type of work, and check the agency's website for opportunities.

Jobs.ca.gov. This website is the place to go for California state government jobs. It has a database that is searchable by county, keywords and other criteria.

Calopps.org. California's cities and public agencies list their job openings here in a database searchable by agency name and city.

Nonprofit job websites

Idealist.org. This organization operates a site where people and nonprofits around the world can exchange ideas, share resources and find employees. Jobs are searchable by country, state and city, and by keywords and areas of focus, which could be anything from disaster relief or health to farming or countless other issues. In addition to job listings, idealist.org includes internships and volunteer opportunities.

Opportunityknocks.org. Opportunity Knocks is an organization dedicated to helping nonprofit organizations find employees and to helping people find jobs in nonprofit organizations. Its database is searchable by location and by job type. The site also has a jobseeker center, where people can post resumes, and a nonprofit resource center, full of articles and tips on how to find a job in that sector.

Specialized job websites

In addition to the websites above, there are also specialized job sites for certain types of businesses.

Hercjobs.org. Higher Education Recruitment Consortium is an excellent example of a specialized job website. The site lists job openings at all its member colleges and universities in northern California, of which there are scores. Jobs vary from professors and vice presidents of development to maintenance workers, carpenters and food service workers.

Allretailjobs.com. This website includes hourly and management jobs ranging from cashiers and clerks to sales executives and transportation/logistics experts. Its listings cover just about all the big names in retail, including Walmart, Costco, Macy's, Toys "R" Us and Pep Boys.

APPENDIX L

The eight most helpful websites

Cacareerzone.org

Career exploration and planning system.

Jailstojobs.org

Information and tools to help ex-offenders find employment. Includes a national directory of free or low cost tattoo removal services and clinics.

Job-hunt.org

Information and links to 13,733 employers and job search resources.

Jobhuntersbible.com

The official online job search resource hosted by Richard Bolles, author of *What Color Is Your Parachute?*

Jobstar.org

Reliable, local information on how to find job openings, community services, company background and job search advice.

Martynemko.com

Packed full of useful articles and information concerning career guidance and landing a job.

Rileyguide.com

Directory of employment and career information sources and services that can be found on the Internet.

Quintcareers.com

Comprehensive expert career and job-hunting advice (through articles, tools, tips, samples and tutorials), as well as links to all the best job sites and professional associations.

APPENDIX M

Using your circle of contacts

The idea of the circle of contacts was created by Larry Robbin, a nationally known expert in the area of workforce development. Here is how he describes it.

Using your circle of contacts.

Picture a bull's eye with your name in the center. Think of the people in your life that you are closest to. These people's names would appear on the first ring out from the center. The next ring would include people who you know but aren't as close to as the first ring. You might include friends in this ring, as well as relatives, neighbors and others. If you keep expanding the circles and fill them with people who you have contact with but may not know very well, you eventually will have your circle of contacts. The full circle of contacts goes way beyond your first circles. Most jobs are found by using your full circle of contacts.

Why is it important to use your circle of contacts?

Most jobs are filled because people had direct contact with the employer. Only a small percentage of people are hired through job postings. Yet most job seekers spend more time on the postings than working toward getting an employer contact. This is because it is easier to look at the Internet than work your circle of contacts. But not finding the right job posting can be depressing. If you talk to two or three people about how they found out about most of the job openings that led to their jobs, you'll usually find out that most of the job information came from personal contacts that led to employers. Working your circle of contacts can be the most effective way to find a job.

I'm not sure I know enough people or the right kind of people to make the circle of contacts work.

Contacts are people who become your eyes and ears during your job search. They aren't the people who have the jobs or do the hiring. Someone you know may hear about a job, see a job opening sign or know people who work in places that may have an opening for you. You want them to give you this information. It can come from any kind of person. It's easy to overlook contacts that could lead to jobs. It's easy to forget all the people who could be used in this circle. This Appendix will help you identify your circle of contacts. The important thing is to remember that contacts are not necessarily people that you know very well. They are contacts, not necessarily friends or people close to you. The person you contact may not have job lead information, but they may know someone who does.

I've tried talking to people about job leads but it hasn't worked.

There are a few different reasons that explain this situation. One is that while working your circle of contacts is one of the most effective job search methods, it is not the only one. This approach should only be one part of your job search strategy. You may get your job leads in another way. Another reason this approach might not be working is that people often don't use their FULL circle of contacts. They don't go out far enough from the center of the bull's eye to use all of their potential contacts. The higher the unemployment rate, the bigger the circles that you have to make. You also need to learn how to work your circle of contacts, not just make the first contact. This involves working the circle of contacts by repeated and varied types of contact. Often when you ask a person once about job information they quickly forget. If you use the ideas in this Appendix about multiple contacts, resumes and JIST cards they will remember your job search needs for a longer period of time.

It's hard for me to talk to people about my job hunting

This is one of the biggest barriers to overcome in using the circle of contacts. It's often very hard for people to talk about being out of work and to ask someone for help. It makes us feel depressed, so we tend to limit these kinds of contacts. This will make our job search last longer, because we're not fully using the circle. Ask your job counselor to help you practice how to talk to people about your job search. If you don't have a job counselor, ask a job counselor at your local American Job Center or community college career center. The more you start working the circle of contacts, the better you will get at this. But it will be hard, especially at the beginning. Remember that working on this problem by using the circles will mean that your job search will end sooner.

To make the circle of contacts work, you should use as many of the following ideas as possible.

1. Use the list of potential contact types in this list. The most common mistake people make is not using big enough circles!
2. When you contact people remember:

A. They may not know of any job openings, but remember to ask them if there is anyone else who they know that you should contact. The circle of contacts gets built on the new contacts that come from this process.

B. Ask the person if they have any job search ideas you should use. How did they get jobs? Be open to new ideas!

C. If anyone gives you a contact or an idea to follow-up on, make sure that you get back to them after you do the follow-up. If people help you and don't hear anything, they assume that you don't need their help anymore. You want to keep them thinking about your job search. Getting back to them, letting them know that you followed their advice and thanking them are good ways of keeping them plugged into your job search. Thank-you notes are a great idea!

D. You need to contact people more than once to get them actively thinking about your job search. Depending on the person, you should contact them at least twice a month. You may want to contact some people more than this. It will also help if you vary the kind of contact. It can be in person, by phone, email, or sending a note via U.S. mail.

E. If you are using a resume or a JIST card, always give several copies to each contact. They need more than one copy to realize that you are serious about them putting your resumes and JIST cards into circulation. Giving people resumes and JIST cards means that they will think about you after the initial contact.

F. Sometimes a conversation with a circle of contacts person may include a variety of topics. Make sure that the conversation ends with you reminding them about your job search needs.

True examples of the circle of contacts in action

1. Tran was looking for work as a truck driver. He gave a copy of his resume to a grocery store owner. The owner showed it to a delivery driver who told him that there was an opening in his company because someone just quit. The company had not put the ad in the paper yet. Tran got the job!

2. Yolanda was working her circle of contacts when she remembered one that she had overlooked. In her old neighborhood she had often babysat for the Patterson family. Yolanda contacted them but nothing happened. When she called back several weeks later, Mr. Patterson admitted that he forgot about her job search but had just found out some information that might be useful to her. He frequently ate lunch in the building cafeteria, and the manager told him that he was considering hiring another waitress. Yolanda asked Mr. Patterson if he would mention her name to the manager. He agreed, and Yolanda followed up with a call, got an interview and got the job!

3. Pete had been looking for a computer job for weeks and thought he had his circle of contacts covered. He had lived in the same neighborhood for 15 years and one day was picking up his dry cleaning from the place he had always gone to when he mentioned his job search to the store owner. There was a computer office in the building above the dry cleaner. The store owner gave him the name of the office manager. Pete called the manager, got referred to another company and eventually got a job!

4. Jose had been out of work for three years after the factory closed. Using the circle of contacts and the phone book, he was able to get in touch with his former foreman. While the foreman had retired, he still belonged to the foreman's association. He circulated Jose's resume at a meeting, and Jose landed a job the following week!

Developing your circle of contacts working list

Use one sheet of paper for each category that applies to your circle of contacts. Think about this carefully—remember to make your network big. Use resumes and JIST cards if possible and re-contact people frequently. You have to activate the circle, and don't assume people will help you unless they get thanked, get feedback on their leads and are re-contacted.

1. Immediate family members.
2. Relatives and extended family members.
3. Friends of family members and relatives.
4. Current neighbors.
5. Former neighbors.

6. Former supervisors.
7. Former co-workers.
8. Small business owners.
9. People in supervisor or manager positions.
10. Union officers.
11. People who have the same hobby you do.
12. Religious leaders.
13. People from recreational, sports, social or cultural activities.
14. Salespeople.
15. Businesses that were connected to your former employer.
16. Caseworkers, social workers, probation or parole officers, and counselors.
17. Politicians.
18. Doctors, lawyers, accountants and tax preparers.
19. People who work in community agencies, government agencies and nonprofits.
20. People in business organizations (neighborhood groups, chambers of commerce and specific types of business associations).
21. People who are active in other kinds of organizations (sports, cultural, community, special groups etc.).
22. Former landlords and real estate agents.
23. People whose jobs put them in places where they may see job leads advertised or hear about jobs: truck drivers, utility or city maintenance workers, waitresses, newspaper carriers, police officers, bartenders, cab drivers, delivery people and many other kinds of people who work outside or in positions working with the public.
24. People who work in a place with many other businesses – malls, industrial parks, office buildings, business parks, etc.
25. People whose jobs take them into other businesses – electricians, repair people, salespeople, food delivery, builders, temporary workers, etc.
26. Mail carriers and postal workers.
27. People from places where you do business – owners and/or employees at the gas station, restaurants, dry cleaner, food store, car repair shop, laundromat, hardware store, bank, pet supply store, hobby stores, childcare provider, entertainment outlet, etc.
28. Retired people who you know.
29. People who you send or say holiday greetings to.
30. People who repair things for you.

31. People who you communicate with on the Internet.
32. Alumni from high school, college, apprenticeships, training programs, etc.
33. People you know from the National Guard or the military.

This list is reprinted with permission from the author Larry Robbin of Robbin and Associates. Robbin and Associates has more than forty-five years of experience providing consulting and training to improve the outcomes of programs serving people in reentry. Nonprofit and government agencies may reprint this list if they include this permission statement. For all other requests to reprint the list or for information about Robbin Associates contact larryrobbin@aol.com.

APPENDIX N

Getting an attitude adjustment

Become a better speaker.

Toastmasters. Toastmasters is an international organization of clubs that meet regularly to learn public speaking and leadership skills. Find your local chapter at www.toastmasters.org.

Practice meditation.

Check out the following for more information on meditation:

Jails to Jobs, Meditation, Why Bother?
www.jailstojobs.org/html/meditation.html
This will give you a taste of mindfulness meditation, including instructions on how to meditate and develop a practice. Click on the link to Doing Your Time with Peace of Mind in the right column. This booklet does a good job of explaining what it is, and can be printed out. It is very useful for both inmates and people on the outside as well.

Center for Mindfulness in Medicine, Health Care and Society.
University of Massachusetts Medical School
www.umassmed.edu/Content.aspx?id=41252

Skillful Means. Resource for people interested in personal growth, overcoming inner obstacles, being helpful to others and expanding consciousness.
http://sites.google.com/site/psychospiritualtools/

Finding a meditation center. For meditation centers in your area check the searchable database at Buddhanet.net, a site that includes meditation centers around the world. You don't have to be a Buddhist, or even religious, to participate in the meditation classes. They're a place to go to learn to meditate for your own wellbeing, to help with stress reduction and to create peace of mind. These classes are usually low-cost or no-cost by donation and usually have a policy of not turning anyone away for lack of funds.

To find one of these classes go to Buddhanet.net, select the World Buddhist directory and click on The Americas, then the state you are in. Put the name of a city in the keyword search and it will give you a list of all the local meditation centers.

APPENDIX O

Money management

An important aspect of reentry is to learn—or relearn—how to deal with money, since it may have been a long time since you were responsible for such things as paying rent or balancing a checkbook.

You may, in fact, come out of prison already in debt from nonpayment of credit cards, child support and/or fees related to the crime you committed, court costs or the services you require. Some reentry programs will offer workshops to help you learn to manage your money. If you can't find a workshop, set up a management system on your own.

The first thing to do if you owe anyone money is to make a list of how much you owe each of them. If you aren't able to make the monthly payments, contact a Credit Counseling Agency. Some of these can be unethical, so it's best to find one through:

- The U.S. Department of Justice, which has database of approved credit counseling agencies listed by state on its website. http://www.justice.gov/ust/eo/bapcpa/ccde/cc_approved.htm.

- The National Federation for Credit Counseling, which has more than 700 nonprofit, community-based agency members in 50 states and Puerto Rico that provide free or low-cost credit counseling. www.nfcc.org.

It's important to set up a budget listing your monthly expenses, including housing, food, transportation, clothing, child expenses, medical care, etc. Try to economize as much as possible and stick to the budget.

Here are three sites to help you learn to manage your money:

1. **www.mymoney.gov** – Run by the U.S. Federal government, it provides information on such things as how to take care of your finances, create a budget and save money.

2. **www.smartaboutmoney.org** – Operated by the National Endowment for Financial Education, it is full of how-to articles and tools to teach people how to create financial goals.

3. **www.mint.com** – This website is for computer savvy people, so that they can organize their accounts, set budgets and create financial goals.

APPENDIX P

Mindfulness and mastery in the workplace: 21 ways to reduce stress during the workday

1. Take five to 30 minutes in the morning to be quiet and meditate. Sit or lie down and be with yourself. Gaze out the window, listen to the sounds of nature or take a slow quiet walk.

2. While your car is warming up try taking a minute to quietly pay attention to your breathing.

3. While driving, become aware of body tension—hands wrapped tightly around the steering wheel, shoulders raised, stomach tight, etc.—and consciously work at releasing and dissolving that tension. Does being tense help you to drive better? What does it feel like to relax and drive?

4. Decide not to play the radio and be with yourself.

5. On the highway, experiment with riding in the right lane, going five miles below the speed limit.

6. Pay attention to your breathing and to the sky, the trees or the quality of your mind when stopped at a red light or toll plaza.

7. Take a moment to orient yourself to your workday once you park your car at your workplace. Use the time walking across the parking lot to step into your life, to know where you are and where you are going.

8. While sitting at your desk, pay attention to bodily sensations, again consciously attempting to relax and rid yourself of excess tension.

9. Use your breaks to truly relax rather than simply "pausing." For instance, instead of having coffee, a cigarette or reading, try taking a short walk or sitting at your desk and renewing yourself.

10. At lunch, changing your environment can be helpful.

11. Try closing your door (if you have one), and take some time to consciously relax.

12. Decide to “STOP” (**S**top, **T**ake a breath, **O**bserve, **P**roceed) for one to three minutes every hour during the workday. Become aware of your breathing and bodily sensations, allowing the mind to settle in as a time to regroup and recoup.

13. Use the everyday cues in your environment—the telephone ringing, sitting at the computer, etc.—as reminders to “center” yourself.

14. Take some time at lunch or other moments in the day to speak with close associates. Try choosing topics that are not necessarily work related.

15. Choose to eat one or two lunches per week in silence. Use this as a time to eat slowly and be with yourself.

16. At the end of the workday, try retracing the day’s activities, acknowledging and congratulating yourself for what you’ve accomplished. Then make a list for tomorrow. You’ve done enough for today!

17. Pay attention to the short walk to your car, breathing the crisp or warm air. Feel the cold or warmth of your body. What might happen if you opened to and accepted these environmental conditions and bodily sensations rather than resisting them? Listen to the sounds outside your workplace. Can you walk without feeling rushed? What happens when you slow down?

18. At the end of the workday, while your car is warming-up, sit quietly, and consciously make the transition from work to home. Take a moment to simply be. Enjoy it for a moment. Like most of us, you’re heading into your next full-time job—home!

19. While driving, notice if you are rushing. What does this feel like? What could you do about it? Remember, you have more control than you might imagine.

20. When you pull into the driveway or park on the street, take a minute to orient yourself to being with your family members or to entering your home.

21. Try changing out of work clothes when you get home. This simple act might help you make a smoother transition into your next "role." Most of the time you can probably spare five minutes to do this. Say hello to each of your family members or to the people you live with. Take a moment to look in their eyes. If possible, take five to 10 minutes to be quiet and still. If you live alone, feel what it is like to enter the quietness of your home, the feeling of entering your own environment.

These ideas come from Saki F. Santorelli, Ed.D., MA, who is the executive director, Center for Mindfulness and assistant professor of medicine at the University of Massachusetts Medical School.

APPENDIX Q

Other resources

Interview Cheat Sheet and Networking Tracker

An organization called Cancer and Careers has created two excellent forms to help you in your job search. Its Interview Cheat Sheet lets you put all of your strengths on paper, so that you will have something to refer to in the interview, in addition to your turnaround talk and turnaround packet.

Cancer and Careers' Networking Tracker helps you keep track of all the people you meet, their details, where you met them and how you followed up. If you know Excel, you can do the same thing on an Excel spreadsheet and then sort it by name, date or other details.

Both the Interview Cheat Sheet and the Networking Tracker are located in the job search section at the bottom of the charts and checklists page on the organization's website at www.cancerandcareers.org/en/resources/charts-and-checklists.

Khan Academy

Make use of Khan Academy's extensive video library, practice exercises and assessments from any computer with access to the web all for free. The video library covers K-12 math; science topics such as biology, chemistry and physics; and even reaches into the humanities with playlists on finance and history. Each of the 4,000-plus videos is a digestible chunk, approximately 10 minutes long, and especially designed for viewing on a computer. Learn more at www.khanacademy.org.

Can't dial 211? Call **800.273.6222** (**TTY** 415.808.4440) or visit us online at **www.211BayArea.org**.

If you are facing a challenge, call 211.
We can help you with:

-Job services

-Food, shelter, clothing and child care

-Rent assistance

-Counseling and health care

-Legal aid

-Senior services

...and so much more!

We can connect you with programs that can save you money.

-Prescription drug discount cards

-Discounted utilities

-Discounted transits passes

-Low-cost auto insurance

-Free and low cost banking services

-Food assistance

Together we'll find options.

211 Bay Area is a service of the Contra Costa Crisis Center, Eden I&R, and United Way of the Bay Area.

FREE • CONFIDENTIAL • MULTI-LINGUAL

*** For 2-1-1 support outside of Bay Area visit www.211us.org**

APPENDIX R

For further reading

Bolles, Richard N. *The Job-Hunter's Survival Guide.* Berkeley, Calif.: Ten Speed Press, 2009.

Bolles, Richard N. *What Color Is Your Parachute?* Berkeley, Calif.: Ten Speed Press, 2013.

Brown, Byron. *Soul without Shame.* Boston: Shambhala Publications, Inc., 1999.

Carnegie, Dale. *How to Stop Worrying and Start Living.* New York: Gallery Books, 2004.

Carnegie, Dale. *How to Win Friends and Influence People.* New York: Pocket Books, 1998.

Cohen, Jeff. *The Complete Idiot's Guide to Recession-Proof Careers.* New York: Alpha Books, 2010.

Enelow, Wendy S. and Krannich, Ronald L. *Best Resumes & Letters for Ex-Offenders.* Manassas Park, Va.: Impact Publications, 2006.

Farr, Michael. *Getting the Job You Really Want.* St. Paul, Minn.: JIST Publishing, 2011.

Farr, Michael and Shatkin, Laurence. *300 Best Jobs Without a Four-Year Degree.* St Paul, Minn.: JIST Publishing, 2009.

Ireland, Susan. *The Complete Idiot's Guide to the Perfect Resume.* New York: Alpha Books, 2010.

Krannich, Caryl and Krannich, Ron. *The Ex-Offenders Job Interview Guide.* Manassas Park, Va.: Impact Publications, 2009.

Krannich, Ron. *The Ex-Offenders Quick Job Hunting Guide.* Manassas Park, Va.: Impact Publications, 2009.

Levinson, Jay Conrad and Perry, David. *Guerrilla Marketing for Job Hunters 3.0.* Hoboken, N.J.: Wiley Publishing, Inc., 2011.

McNulty, Neil P. and Krannich, Ronald L. *The Ex-Offenders 30/30 Job Solution.* Manassas Park, Va.: Impact Publications, 2009.

Nemko, Marty. *Cool Careers For Dummies.* Hoboken, N.J.: Wiley Publishing, Inc., 2007.

Richardson, Simone R. *The Zen of Resume Writing for Formerly Incarcerated Persons.* Bloomington, Ind.: iUniverse, Inc., 2007.

Schneider, Glen. *Ten Breaths to Happiness: Touching Life in its Fullness.* Berkeley, Calif.: Parallax Press, 2013.

Stahl, Bob and Goldstein, Elisha. *A Mindfulness-Based Stress Reduction Workbook.* Alameda, Calif.: New Harbinger Publications, 2010.

Your feedback is critical

We want to make the work we do as relevant and useful as possible to those in reentry. The only way we can do that is with your feedback. We'd like to know which of the things we wrote about in this book are most helpful to you and if there is anything we didn't include that you feel you need to know.

Please go to our website and tell us what you think by answering some questions. We are also interested in hearing your success stories and the challenges you are facing in your search for employment. It will only take a few minutes of your time but may make a difference in the way we present our material. You can find the questionnaire at www.jailstojobs.org.

If you or anyone you know would like to support our pre-release and reentry efforts, please visit jailstojobs.org to make a donation. We would be grateful if you did.

INDEX

D

E

J

Q

R

Y

NOTES

NOTES

NOTES

NOTES